ics

Unit 3

igital imaging–plan and produce

Unit 5

desktop publishing

Anne Kelsall
Graham Manson
Ruksana Patel
Steve Cushing

Consultant: Keith Parry

OCR level 2
Nationals
ict

www.harcourt.co.uk

✓ Free online support
✓ Useful weblinks
✓ 24 hour online ordering

01865 888070

PAYNE-GALLWAY

Payne-Gallway is an imprint of Pearson Education Limited, a company incorporated in England and Wales, having its registered office at Edinburgh Gate, Harlow, Essex, CM20 2JE. Registered company number: 872828

www.payne-gallway.co.uk

First published 2007

12 11 10 09 08 07
10 9 8 7 6 5 4 3 2 1

British Library Cataloguing in Publication Data is available from the British Library on request.

ISBN 978 1 905292 15 8

Designed by Kamae Design
Produced and Typeset by Sparks, Oxford – www.sparks.co.uk
Printed by Printer Trento S.r.l
Cover photo/illustration © Steve Shott

Acknowledgements
Microsoft product screenshots reprinted with permission from Microsoft Corporation.

Adobe and Macromedia® product screenshots reprinted with permission from Macromedia.

All photographs used in this book are reproduced courtesy of the authors.

Every effort has been made to contact copyright holders of material reproduced in this book. Any omissions will be rectified in subsequent printings if notice is given to the publishers.

The websites used in this book were correct and up-to-date at the time of publication. It is essential for tutors to preview each website before using it in class so as to ensure that the URL is still accurate, relevant and appropriate. We suggest that tutors bookmark useful websites and consider enabling students to access them through the school/college intranet.

Ordering Information
Payne-Gallway, FREEPOST (OF1771),
PO Box 381, Oxford OX2 8BR
Tel: 01865 888070
Fax: 01865 314029
Email: orders@payne-gallway.co.uk

Contents

Series Introduction

Introduction

This book is one of a series of books that has been designed to guide you in your work for OCR Level 2 Nationals in ICT. Each book covers two or three units and explains the skills and concepts that are needed for each. It also sets out in detail how to create a portfolio to achieve a **Pass**, **Merit** or **Distinction** for each assessment objective.

How to use this book

This book is divided into two sections which guide you through each Assessment Objective (AO) as set out by OCR in the specifications for Unit 3 and Unit 5. Every chapter helps you to understand how you would build evidence for your portfolio through a clear Scenario, helpful Tips and structured Activities, using step-by-step instructions. At every stage clear guidance is given as to the level of evidence required for a **Pass**, **Merit** or **Distinction** so that you are able to plan your own progress effectively.

Work through the chapters in sequence. Read all the explanations and work through the sections explaining the skills. Carry out each activity making sure you save all files as you complete the activities.

To help you, examples are provided in the Units 3 & 5 Student Resources folder which can be downloaded from the OCR Nationals in ICT (Units 3 & 5) Student Resources page on the Payne-Gallway website (**www.payne-gallway.co.uk**).

Symbols used in this book

→ means that a new instruction follows or an option from a menu or sub-menu should be selected.

Example: **Edit** → **Copy** means click **Edit** on the menu bar, then click **Copy**.

The practice assignments

These assignments are provided to help you practise the skills required for the units in this book.

UNIT 3

Digital Imaging

In this unit you will cover the following...

- **AO1** **Describe and evaluate a range of bitmap and vector images**
- **AO2** **Plan the production of graphic images for a client**
- **AO3** **Source and store components for graphic products**
- **AO4** **Record the sources of computer graphics and consider relevant legislation**
- **AO5** **Use appropriate software tools to create, edit and combine graphic images**
- **AO6** **Present work to a client for a specific purpose, using a suitable format for display**

CHAPTER 1

Assessment Objective 1

Describe and Evaluate a Range of Bitmap and Vector Images

Overview:

Before you produce graphics and images, you need to carry out research into existing graphics and images. This research will help you to decide on a range of issues, such as content, purpose and audience of the graphics and images you create.

This Assessment Objective focuses upon the research you need to carry out to find suitable graphics and images. Once you have found a range of graphics and images, you will then analyse them so that you can identify audience and purpose, the message, if any, which the graphic or image conveys, the medium and size of the graphic or image, as well as how effective the graphic or image is. In this chapter, you will be shown how to decide on which images to analyse and how these may be collected. We will also discuss how you may describe each of the graphics and images you collect.

How this assessment objective will be assessed...

You will be assessed on the following aspects of your work:

- The amount of graphics and images you collect.
- The number of sources you use to collect a range of images.
- The quality and range of information you provide in your description of the graphics and images you collect.

Skills to use...

This is a 'research and describe' Assessment Objective. Your first task will be to plan so that you find at least one graphic from three of the four sources. Even if you are aiming at a **Pass** in this unit, it is still a good idea to complete this section well as it gives you the skills and understanding you will need to complete the other Assessment Objectives in this unit.

One skill you need is the power of description. Great descriptions will start with a very clear understanding of the purpose of any graphics you choose. If you can be clear about why the graphic has been chosen, you then have a better chance of describing and criticising the graphic as necessary.

How to achieve...

Pass requirements

P1 You will collect and display a range of graphics from two different sources.

P2 You will describe the purpose of the graphics you have collected.

P3 You will comment on the suitability of the graphics you have collected.

Merit requirements

M1 You will collect and display examples of graphics from three different sources.

M2 You will describe the graphics you have collected. This description will include:

- the purpose of each graphic
- the audience of each graphic
- the suitability of the graphics.

M3 You will indicate the size of some of the graphics discussed.

Distinction requirements

D1 You will collect and display examples of graphics from three different sources.

D2 You will describe the graphics you have collected. This description will include:

- the purpose of each graphic
- the audience of each graphic
- the suitability for purpose of each graphic
- the message, if any, conveyed by each graphic
- how effective, or ineffective, each graphic is.

D3 You will indicate the size of most of the graphics discussed.

Software

There are many different art packages you could use to complete your work for this unit. We will be working with Macromedia® Fireworks®, which includes a wide range of tools and features but which is relatively easy to use to achieve great effects. Do not worry if you are going to use a different software application because a lot of the work we cover will be extremely useful to you.

Graphics and images

When working with what some people may call 'pictures', you need to make sure that everyone understands the terms you will use. You cannot use the term 'pictures' because it is too vague and is not really the technical term. We will use the term 'graphics' to mean any images that may otherwise be called 'pictures'.

Key term

Computer graphic

Any form of image which may be shown on a computer.

Researching graphics

You will need to collect a range of graphics from three different sources. Once you have collected your graphics, you will then go on to describe and evaluate them, using the techniques we will discuss below. In the next section, we will discuss the range of sources from which you may collect graphics. If you are targeting either a **Merit** or **Distinction** grade, you must use graphics from **three** of the sources listed. Do not worry though, you only need to use one graphic from each source.

Sources of graphics

There are four main areas from which you could collect graphics. These are shown below, along with further explanation if necessary.

- **Graphics printed on paper**. These include graphics which may be found in news-papers/magazines, advertisements and posters.
- **Graphics printed on other surfaces**. These include graphics which may be found on packaging, labels or signs.
- **Graphics viewed on screen**. These include digital artwork, such as buttons, icons, banners and images which may be found on websites, as well as backgrounds which may be found in a range of software types and formats.
- **Technical graphics**. These include maps, diagrams and plans.

Activity 1: Researching graphics...

In this activity you will find and describe graphics.

You have been asked to produce a portfolio of graphics. You will use this portfolio to help plan which graphics to include in a forthcoming project. Your first task will be to gather these graphics from three of the four sources mentioned above.

- Using any planning method you wish, decide on the graphics you will find.
- Gather your graphics. Make a note of where you found them. We will be looking below at how to use the graphics you discover. You may want to jump ahead and check the next section if you want to complete this task in one go.

Vector and bitmap images

The sections below all explain the different headings under which you should describe your graphics. However, before we carry on, we need to discuss the difference between vector and bitmap graphics.

You will probably have come across bitmap and vector graphics in other ICT lessons. However, a quick reminder may be a good idea.

Bitmap graphics are made up of many small dots each individually coloured to make up the overall image. Each dot is called a **pixel**. As you enlarge a bitmap image, so each pixel of the image becomes bigger on the screen. This results in the effect called **pixelation**, where an image loses quality as it becomes bigger.

Vector graphics are saved as a series of instructions that make up shapes within a graphic. These instructions are basically mathematical formulas that control the location and characteristics of the shape. These formulas are recalculated when you resize the graphic, so vector graphics do not lose quality like bitmap graphics.

Key terms

Bitmap graphic

A graphic image created by storing details about pixels included in the image.

Vector graphic

A graphic image created by storing details of the magnitude and direction of lines that make up shapes within an image.

Pixelation

The effect caused by displaying an image at such a magnification that the eye can pick out individual pixels.

Describing graphics

Once you have collected your suitable graphics, you will need to describe and evaluate each of them. If you are aiming at a **Pass**, you should describe graphics from two sources and your description should include:

- the purpose of the graphic
- the suitability of the graphic.

If you are aiming for a **Merit**, you should describe a range of graphics from three different sources and your description should include:

- the purpose of the graphic
- the audience for the graphic
- the suitability of the graphic
- the size of some of the graphics.

If you are aiming for a **Distinction**, you should describe a range of graphics from three different sources and your description should include:

- the purpose of the graphic
- the audience for the graphic
- the suitability of the graphic
- the message being conveyed by the graphic
- the size of most of the graphics.

For a **Distinction**, you should also comment on whether or not the graphics are effective.

What is a range of graphics?

The *Guidance on assessment and evidence requirements* section of the specification states that:

> *When collecting graphics from the different sources listed, they need only use one graphic from each.*

This is therefore saying that for each source of graphic you use, such as 'graphics printed on paper', you need to have only one graphic.

Audience and purpose

For **Merit** and **Distinction** grades, part of the basic description of your graphic needs to be a description of the target audience. You will probably have come across this term in other books in this series. However, if you have not, here is a quick explanation.

'Target audience' is a very important concept, as it is the group of people at which a product is aimed. For a general product, such as a type of food eaten by a wide range of people, there would be a very large target audience. An example of such a product may be burgers sold in a chain of restaurants. Many different types of people will eat such food and so the advertising and publicity for this product need to be quite general. However, for other products, such as specialist books, there will be a very narrow target audience, as only people who are interested in the subject matter for this book would buy it. An example of this may be books of locomotive numbers published for train-spotters. Any train-spotters reading this book will now be shouting that this is not a narrow interest and there are thousands of people who share the hobby. However, even the keenest train-spotter will accept that there are more people who eat burgers than spot trains and so will accept that the book, as well as any advertising, must appeal to that relatively narrow target audience.

Key term

Target audience

The group of people to which something (in this case a graphic) is intended to appeal.

Graphics used in magazines or on packaging are not chosen at random, but are the result of a selection process which whittles graphics down from a large choice to a final few which all suit the article or product or purpose for which they are being used. You need to develop the ability to choose the most suitable graphic for your work. Describing the purpose of graphics used by other people is an important stage in developing this skill.

Graphics can be used for many different purposes. Some are listed below:

- To make a point.
- To clarify a point or explanation.
- To give an example.
- To shock.
- To entertain.
- To attract attention.

Graphics may also be used because of the role they play on the page. For example, they may be used to break up text on a page so that the page looks more interesting. However, while this may be one purpose of the graphic, the choice of which graphic to use will be based on the same criteria as any other graphic used.

When you come to decide on the purpose of a graphic, try to get a feel for the context in which the graphic is used. This may include reading the text or looking at other images used in the same context.

Suitability for purpose

We have already explained that the choice of which graphic to use on a page will be the result of a long selection process. However, this process does not always identify the most suitable graphic. Your task is to make a decision about how suitable the graphics you describe are for their purpose. Obviously, this will depend on how well you have identified the purpose. If the purpose you describe is not quite the same as the purpose which was originally identified, you may have a problem. However, it is probably better to ignore this possibility and assume that you have correctly identified the purpose.

The suitability of the graphic is therefore the simple question of whether the graphic is the best for the job. For example, the subject matter of the graphic may be poorly chosen or the quality of the graphic itself may be poor. In both these cases, you may decide that the graphic is not as suitable for purpose as you would expect. As you shall see, there is a subtle difference between the suitability of a graphic and how effective it is.

Message conveyed

Graphics can be used to convey messages. Some of these messages are very clear (for example, someone showing fear or great joy). Other messages may be more subtle and are obvious only if you know what you are looking for. At this level, you only really need to be looking for the obvious messages which may be included in a graphic. These may be human emotions, such as fear or joy, but they may simply be warnings, such as 'do not play on railway lines' or 'do not throw fireworks'. However, to cover all possibilities, the specification for this unit is very clear that it is possible for a graphic not to convey a message, so you do not have to have a message for everything. If you feel that a graphic does not have a message, say so.

Medium used for the graphic

The medium used for a graphic will basically be one of the four sources of graphics explained above. For a graphic from the group called **graphics printed on paper**, the medium is paper. However, you may decide to give slightly more information than this. For example, you may wish to explain that a particular graphic was on glossy high-quality paper, while another was on poor-quality newsprint paper. Similarly, for a graphic from the group called **graphics viewed on screen**, you could simply state that the graphic was found online and therefore the medium was a computer screen. However, you could go on to state that the graphic was found on a website or in a slideshow presentation.

Size of the graphic

The graphic size could describe the physical size of the graphic on the page or the actual size of the graphic file. The physical size could give the percentage of the page which the graphic covers or the actual dimensions of the graphic (which are found by measuring the graphic with a ruler).

If you have used other Macromedia® applications, such as Macromedia® Flash®, you will not be surprised to find that Fireworks® has a **Properties** panel at the bottom of the screen which shows information about the graphic on which you are working.

Figure 1.1: *The Properties panel.*

A simple way of finding the file size of a graphic is to hover the mouse over the file icon in Windows Explorer. After a short period of time, the file size of the graphic will appear.

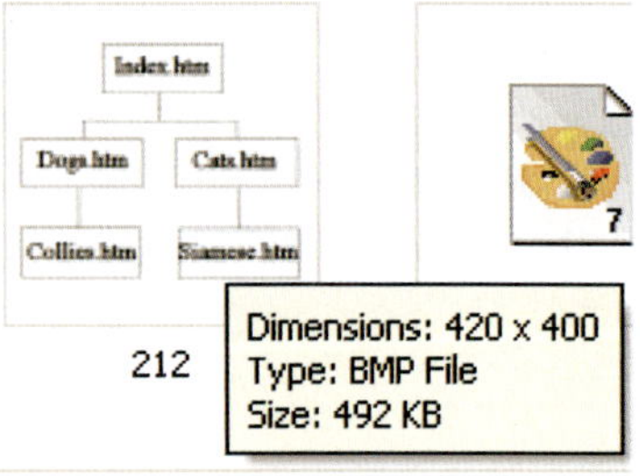

Figure 1.2: *Using Windows Explorer to display the file size.*

Effectiveness of the product

Do not confuse **suitability** and **effectiveness**. While the two terms are quite close in meaning, the issue here is about whether the graphic chosen is effective. It is possible that an unsuitable graphic (that is one which may not contain quite the subject matter you may expect) can be effective. This may be because the graphic chosen may, for example, be pixelated, and so is not as suitable as a clear well-presented graphic, yet the message which the graphic is meant to convey is clear for the task which it is meant to complete.

When you come to discuss a graphic, especially if you are targeting a **Distinction** grade, be sure to consider both its suitability (describing how well chosen the graphic is) as well as its effectiveness (describing how well it does the job for which it was chosen).

Displaying and referencing your graphics

Activity 2: Describe graphics...

In this activity you will describe the graphics you gathered in Activity 1.

Describe the graphics you have gathered. You should be aware that the different grades for this qualification require different descriptions of the graphics. Your description should suit your target grade for this qualification.

The final area we must discuss is how to reference your graphics. For resources which you find on the World Wide Web, a URL showing the location of the graphic, as well as a print out or screenshot of the graphic, would be appropriate. For other graphics you could either use a scanner or digital camera to capture a digital copy of the original graphic. A final option may be to simply include the originals with the work, either by cutting them out of the magazines or newspapers where you have found them or, in the case of packaging or labels, you could include the whole of the graphic.

CHAPTER 2

Assessment Objective 2

Plan the Production of Graphic Images for a Client

Overview:

This chapter leads on from the research you did in the previous chapter. You will learn how to plan a range of graphics. The quality of your plans, including the detail, will decide the grade you achieve for this Assessment Objective. However, remember that when you produce your own work for this unit, the graphics you plan, and then produce, must have been created using a wide range of bitmap and vector tools. While you are not directed to produce a fixed number of graphics, you will need to plan and produce sufficient graphics to cover this requirement.

How this assessment objective will be assessed...

You will be assessed on the following aspects of your work:

- The amount of detail you include in your plans, including deadlines for completion.
- The amount of supporting detail for each of the plans you produce. This should include:
  - your ideas from initial research
  - the purpose of a graphic
  - the target audience for a graphic
  - where the graphic will be used
  - the size, resolution and file format for each file.

Skills to use...

- Your designs should show accuracy and imagination.
- You will need to show a good understanding of the purpose of graphics.

How to achieve...

Pass requirements

P1 You will describe the purpose and audience of the graphics that are to be created.

P2 You will plan the graphics to be created, using rough sketches which identify some of the key areas.

Merit requirements

M1 You will describe the purpose and audience of the graphics that are to be created. Your description may refer to ideas which you gained when doing your research for AO1 of this unit.

M2 You will plan the graphics to be created, using rough sketches which identify most of the key areas.

Distinction requirements

D1 You will describe the purpose and audience of the graphics that are to be created.

D2 You will discuss where the graphics will be used and will also identify size, resolution and file format for each graphic. Your description may refer to ideas which you gained when doing your research for AO1 of this unit.

D3 You will set deadlines for your work.

D4 You will plan the graphics to be created, using rough sketches which identify all of the key areas.

Describing the graphics that you will create

Once you have completed your research into graphics, you should have a clearer idea about the type of graphics which you will produce. However, before you dive in and create your graphics, you will need to plan them. As part of that planning, you will need to produce sketch plans.

Sketch plans

TIP

It is a good idea to have a look at Assessment Objective 5 before you begin your planning. You will need to plan and create both vector and bitmap graphics which use a wide range of tools. Assessment Objective 5 lists some of the tools you could use. As you will see, there are quite a few.

Throughout this chapter, you will be asked to create sketch plans or diagrams. You do not need to use software for these plans; a pen and paper will do. The difference between each of the grade bands is the detail you include with your plans. The rest of this chapter deals with the detail you need to include, rather than how to draw nice pictures. This is because nice pictures will not get you good grades, but good planning and lots of relevant detail will.

Relevant detail

When you describe the graphics you are going to create, you will need to describe a range of features of your graphics. These features are:

- the target audience
- the purpose
- where the graphic will be used
- the size, resolution and file format.

You should also include:

- ideas from initial research
- deadlines.

We discussed the target audience, purpose and size of graphics in Chapter 1. You should go back now to refresh your understanding of these concepts, if you are unsure of them, as they are very important to your success in this unit.

We will now discuss the remaining concepts.

Where will the graphics be used?

You will be planning a range of computer graphics. One of the issues, about which you need to be clear, is where each graphic is to be used. This is important, because where a graphic will be used should influence how it is made. For example, a main graphic at the top of a page may be a high-resolution, colour graphic with plenty of detail, while a smaller graphic used halfway down the page, or used as a button on a website, may be black and white and be of relatively low resolution. Therefore, before you plan your graphics, you need to consider the location. To some extent, this is linked to the purpose of the graphic, since a main banner graphic is likely to be at the top of the page, while a minor graphic will probably be anywhere *but* at the top of the page.

As well as indicating the location on a page of the graphic, you should also identify whether the graphic is to be used on a page, a website or a presentation. As you shall see, this can affect other design considerations.

Graphic resolution

Resolution is how many pixels are used in a bitmap image and is usually set at an amount per inch, such as 72 dpi, which means that the image has 72 dots per inch. Resolution is set when a bitmap graphic is first created.

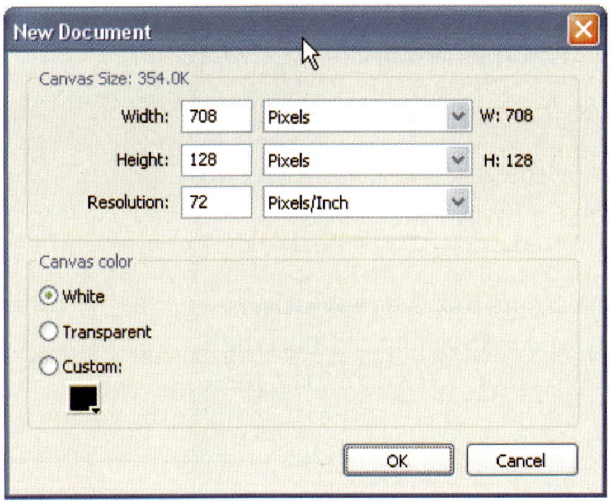

Figure 2.1: *The resolution setting for a new Fireworks® graphic.*

Key term

Resolution

The number of dots used in a bitmap graphic.

You should realise that, as all bitmap graphics are made up of dots, the number of dots you use will affect the quality of your graphic. Obviously, if you use a low resolution, such a 10 dpi, you will have trouble trying to show great detail. Imagine you are viewing a curve. Because you would have very few dots per inch, your graphic would have very rough edges, as the curve would have to be shown over a very few dots. However, if you were using a higher resolution (more dots per inch, such as 300), there are more available so each dot would have to show less of the curvature change.

Another consideration might be the cost of printing. Higher resolution means more dots per inch, which means more ink is required. However, this is probably something you can ignore at this stage.

Another consideration is file size. If you increase the amount of dots which make up a bitmap graphic, then you increase the amount of data which makes up the graphic.

Finally, we come to the biggest consideration when working with resolution and this is the area where purpose and location come into play. If you are trying to create graphics, you will probably want your graphics to be of as good a quality as possible. On paper, it is usually argued that the resolution needs to be at least 300 dpi for the individual dots not to be noticed by the naked eye. However, when working with graphics for use on the Web, a resolution of 72 dpi is considered sufficient.

In the next activity, you will create two Fireworks® files and be introduced to two Fireworks® tools. These two tools are the **Line tool** and the **Freeform tool**. The Line tool's role is obvious – it is used to draw lines. The Freeform tool can be used to distort lines to make curves from straight lines. Once you have drawn a line, you can then select the Freeform tool and click on the line. Continue to press the left-hand mouse button and you can drag the line to create an 'S' shape or something more complicated.

The next activity also introduces you to the **Preview** feature.

Figure 2.2: *The Original, Preview and split screen display choices.*

Activity 1: Investigating resolution...

In this activity you will explore the effects of using different resolution settings.

- Open Fireworks® and create a new graphic. You can do this in one of two ways:
  - Either click the **Create New Fireworks File** option on the welcome splash screen which is displayed when you launch Fireworks®, or
  - Select **File** → **New**.
- In the dialogue box that is displayed (see Figure 2.1) make sure that the **resolution** units are set to Pixels/Inch (this is the same as dpi) and type a resolution of 5 dpi. The width and height of your graphic are not important at this stage, as long as they are not too small.
- Click the OK button to show your new blank canvas.
- Use the **Line tool** to draw a line from the top left of your canvas to the bottom right.
- Use the **Freeform tool** to distort the line into an S.
- Click the **Preview** button; you will see that your line is very lumpy or jumpy, especially on the curves. It is not a high-quality line.
- Repeat the steps above, but this time use a resolution of 300 dpi.

File format

You will probably already have come across a range of different file types. You can tell a file type by looking at the full filename. The file extension (the letters after the full stop) indicate the file type, so for a graphics file, e.g. **Paris.bmp**, the .bmp extension tells you that the file is a bitmap file.

There are different file types of bitmap and vector graphics. Bitmap graphic file types are usually .jpg, .bmp and .gif, although you may easily come across some others, such as .png, .raw and .tif. These are all general file types and each has specific properties of which you must be aware if you are to choose the most appropriate file type for a graphic.

As well as these main six types, you may come across some which are file types associated with one piece of software only, for example Corel's Paint Shop Pro uses .psp files, and Adobe Photoshop uses .psd files.

Vector graphic files are usually Scalable Vector Graphic (.svg) files but you may come across Encapsulated PostScript (.eps) files.

Choosing a bitmap file type

Whether you are working with bitmap or vector graphics, you will usually want a file type which stores your work in as small a file as possible, yet still gives you a good image when opened. You will also want a file type which suits the purpose of your graphic. If you are producing graphics for use on the Web, you should use .jpg, .gif or .png file types, as these are the ones which most browsers can use. If you use a different file type, a web browser might display your graphic incorrectly.

As you now know, the resolution of a bitmap graphic affects file size, but you will also need to make a decision about file **compression** as this also determines size and quality. Compression is the process of making a graphic file smaller. This reduction in file size is usually achieved by reducing the amount of data held in the file. As this data is information held about the graphic, reducing data means a reduction in information held about the file (**lossy** compression). Data loss is sometimes achieved by cutting down the number of colours used in the graphic. In most cases, this is usually so subtle that you do not notice. However, if you use very high levels of compression, you will start to notice a reduction in quality. (**Lossless** compression reduces file size by using complicated mathematics, but all the graphic information is kept.)

Key terms

Compression

Decreasing the file size.

Compression ratio

The ratio between the file size of the original graphic and the compressed graphic.

Lossless compression

Keeps all the information (by using maths) in a file when it is compressed and so does not reduce quality.

Lossy compression

Loses information (e.g. colours) in a file when it is compressed and so reduces quality.

Hints and tips

The next table gives some hints and tips about which graphic file type to choose.

File type	Advantages	Disadvantages
.bmp	This format was developed by Microsoft and is very widely supported.	Files can be very large and some applications do not support compression.
.gif	This is a great file type if you want a graphic which uses only 256 colours. Suitable for graphics on web pages.	Photographs use more than 256 colours and require lossy compression.
.jpg	Very good compression ratios can be achieved with little loss of quality.	Lossy compression occurs every time you save a graphic, therefore data is lost at every save.
.png	Good compression ratios with no loss of information.	Large file sizes, despite compression being applied.
.raw	Comes free with some digital cameras. Can achieve reasonably good compression ratios.	Can only be opened if you have the correct software.
.tif	Suitable for lossless compression so great for working on files.	Large file size.

Probably your best option is to use a file type with lossless compression while working on your files and, once you have completed all of the necessary work, then choose one of the file types which allows lossy compression.

Choosing vector file types

Both .svg and .eps formats are mentioned above, but it is probably better to choose the .svg format, as this is widely used and is extremely flexible.

Planning your computer graphics

The graphics you produce for this unit will be for a set client with set needs. However, when you are planning which graphics to produce, you need to remember that you must meet the requirements of Assessment Objective 5, one of which is to use a wide range of bitmap and vector tools. It is therefore very important that you plan to create sufficient graphics for you to use a wide range of tools from **both** bitmap and vector graphic packages.

To help you, the syllabus gives a list of components which you should include in your plans for the graphics you will produce. Some of the ones which we have not yet covered are:

- lines (using different style and thickness)
- text (using different fonts, sizes and colours)
- basic shapes
- colour
- paper size and orientation.

We will deal with how to use these tools in Chapter 5, but for now, you need to know how each can be used in the design process. Some of what follows may seem obvious, but there will also be some information here which you will not have come across before. You should read the information below and use the software to get a better idea of the range of possibilities available to you before you start to design your graphics.

Lines

Fireworks® gives you a great deal of control over how any lines you draw appear. You can control the amount of ink which is used to create the line, the size and tip of the pen, the edge effect, the colour and even the texture of the line. Each of these options is set in the **Line properties** panel.

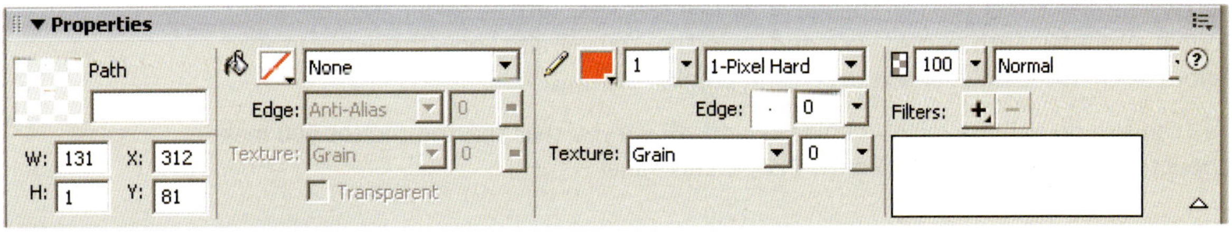

Figure 2.3: *The Line properties panel.*

Options such as the **Tip size** or **Edge softness** are set by using a slider. However, the **Stroke category** and **Texture** menus provide a list of options. The **Stroke category** options are shown below.

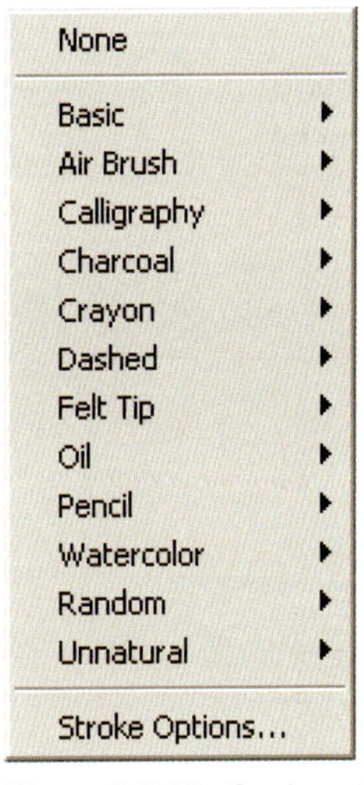

Figure 2.4: *The Stroke category options.*

Text

If you have used a word processor, you will know that there is a wide range of different fonts available to choose from. Fonts are groups of letters that have a common design (i.e. what the letters looks like). Choosing which fonts to use is another example of making sure a 'look' suits the intended purpose. This page is written in a font which is considered to be easy to read because it is simple and not fussy. However, a font that looks like handwriting would not be suitable for official documents, such as bank statements, because it is very hard to read.

You also need to know that some fonts are 'scalable'. This means that if they are part of a graphic that needs to be made larger, the font will increase in size without the obvious pixelation you would expect to see with a bitmapped font. However, it is always better to use a font that suits the size of the final graphic, as this will always look better on the page.

You will be aware that you can change other text features, such as colour and size, and format attributes, such as bold, italic and underline. You will also know that you can alter layout, such as setting your text to be centrally aligned.

You can also do all these things within Fireworks®. As you shall see, the choices you make about text are, again, made using the **Properties** panel.

Basic shapes

Basic shapes are circles, squares, rectangles and triangles and any other non-complex shape. If you think about a graphic, most can be made up using a few basic shapes. As you become a better artist, so these shapes may become less basic, or perhaps better merged so that you cannot tell that a complex shape started off as combination of simple components. In design work, you may actually do a good deal of work with basic shapes, however good you become at your art.

When you are planning your artwork, using basic shapes as part of the design will allow you to plan how graphics fit together on the page and also how the graphics themselves may be constructed.

Figure 2.5: *A house drawn using basic rectangles.*

Colour

There are many different colours available in Fireworks®. The colours you choose are important and affect your design. You will be shown how to select colours in Chapter 5.

Paper size and orientation

Paper size is the dimensions of the sheet of paper with which you are working. Paper size should not be confused with the physical size of the graphic. The size of the graphic is set when the graphic is created, whereas the paper size is the dimensions of the paper on which the graphic will be placed.

Paper orientation is whether the paper has it longest side as the vertical edge (**portrait** orientation) or as its horizontal edge (**landscape** orientation).

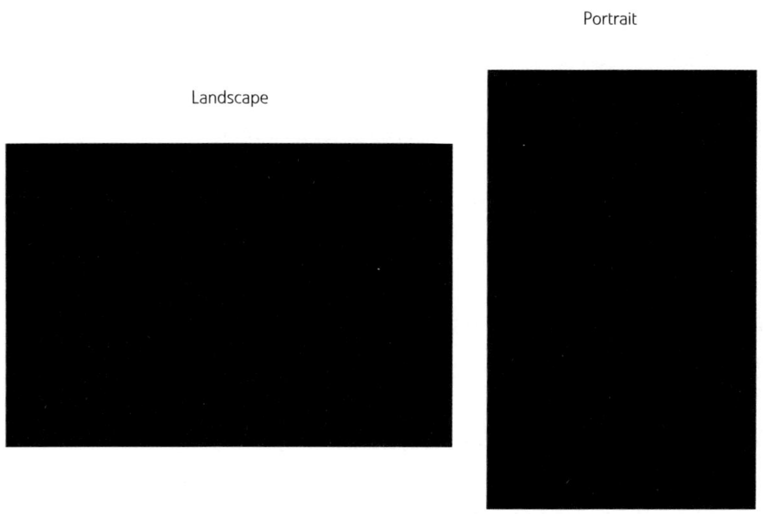

Figure 2.6: *Landscape and portrait orientation.*

And finally

The final part of your planning should be to refer back to the ideas you got from your research for Assessment Objective 1. Hopefully, the graphics you evaluated as part of your work for this Assessment Objective will have given you loads of ideas which you want to include in your graphics. Now is the time to use these ideas. If you include ideas from your research, it is a good idea to reference your research. If, for example, you found a really clever use of background graphics in a document, you could include a note such as:

Set out the background like in sample graphic A

This would make it clear to everyone that you have used your research to help decide how your graphics will appear.

You also need to set yourself deadlines for your work. This can be as simple as producing a list of tasks and setting dates by which time each task will be completed.

CHAPTER 3

Assessment Objective 3

Source and Store Components for Graphic Products

Overview:

In this chapter, we will look at how you can find and then store the parts you will eventually use to create your graphics. These parts may be whole graphics, which you then combine with other graphics, or parts of graphics. We will look at a range of different sources and, for each source, show how you can store the graphics you choose to use.

You are strongly advised to complete the work for this Assessment Objective alongside the work for Assessment Objective 4.

How this assessment objective will be assessed...

You will be assessed on the following aspects of your work:

- The range of sources from which you access graphics.
- The relevance of the graphics you use.

Skills to use...

This unit is about choosing from where you source your graphics as well as the graphics you use. When you plan your work, think of as wide a range of different places from which you could obtain graphics as you can. This range of sources will lead you into making decisions about which graphics you use. This decision making will automatically involve considering whether the graphics you choose are relevant to your work.

How to achieve...

Pass requirements

P1 You will source and store graphics from two of the possible source areas listed on page 19.

P2 Some of your graphics may not be appropriate.

Merit requirements

M1 You will source and store graphics from three of the possible source areas listed on page 19.

M2 Most of your graphics will be appropriate.

Distinction requirements

D1 You will source and store graphics from all of the possible source areas listed below.

D2 All of your graphics will be appropriate.

The assignment for this unit

The work you produce for this unit will be based on a commission from two comedians, Les Gets and Des Trunks. Les and Des were huge stars in the 1970s and filled concert halls throughout the United Kingdom, though they never played abroad. Their style was very much based on what they had learned playing the clubs in the North of England. At one stage, they had a television series called *Up North with Les and Des*, which allowed them to show their unique brand of humour to a wider audience.

Unfortunately tastes change, and Les and Des did not survive the wave of alternative comedy which grew up at the end of the 1970s. However, they now feel the time is right for a comeback. They have booked a number of venues and now want a series of graphics to help publicise their forthcoming tour. You will be producing the artwork for these elements. As we explained in Chapter 1, you will be working with Macromedia® Fireworks® to produce these elements. In this chapter, you will be gathering elements which will be used to create some of these graphics.

Sources of graphics

A range of different graphic sources are provided in the syllabus. These are organised into three categories as follows:

- Computer graphics – these are graphics you find on the World Wide Web or in a clipart library. Not all clipart comes from websites.
- Graphics captured by a digital camera.
- Graphics which are scanned onto a computer.

Remember: If you are aiming at a **Pass** grade, you will need to use graphics from two of these categories. For a **Merit** grade you will need to use graphics from three categories and for a **Distinction** grade you will need to use graphics from all three categories and include computer graphics from clipart galleries and the WWW.

As mentioned in the overview section, the graphics for your assignment can either be whole graphics which you manipulate using Fireworks® or you can select areas of graphics for the same treatment.

Saving graphics

This unit is about gathering graphics with which you will work later. As you have learnt in Unit 1, it is a good idea if your work area is organised using suitably named folders/directories. If you have a folder for Unit 3, you should navigate to that folder and then save your graphic there. You may even want to create another folder/directory especially for graphics in the Unit 3 folder/directory and save your images there.

If you do not have a folder/directory set up for your Unit 3 work, then create one now. It will make it far easier for you to organise your work.

Sourcing graphics from the Web

The Web is a great source of graphics, but you need to be aware that many graphics found there are subject to the **Copyright, Designs and Patents Act (1988)**. This Act gives the creator or owner of a graphic control over how and where the graphic is used. We will be looking more closely at how this Act affects you in Chapter 4.

Activity 1: Selecting, saving and copying graphics from the Web...

In this activity you will learn how to save and copy graphics you find on the Web.

Les and Des would like a range of photographs of countryside from the North of England as a background for their tour poster. They have asked you to find a selection which may be used.

As a group:

- decide on the criteria you will use to choose your graphics
- decide on the criteria you will use to search the Web for suitable graphics.

Individually:

- Open your web browser and navigate to your favourite search engine. Use the criteria you have decided on to find a suitable graphic.
- **Copy** this graphic to your work area by clicking the right-hand mouse button on the graphic you wish to save. The graphics context menu is displayed. Choose **Save picture as...** .
- You will be taken to the default location for your graphics – this will probably be a folder called **My Pictures**. Navigate to your **Unit 3** folder and save the image there.

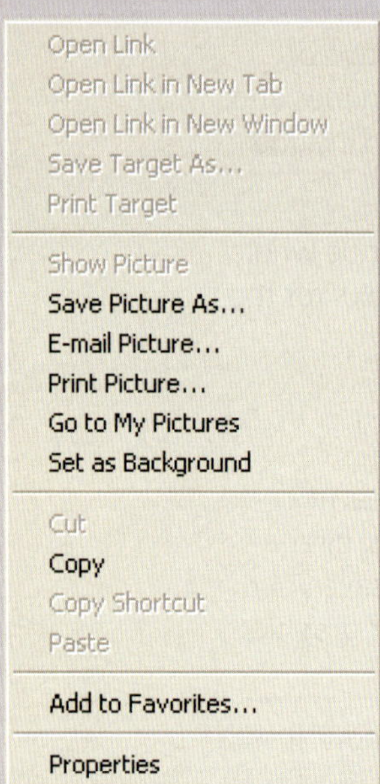

Figure 3.1: *The graphics context menu.*

TIP

We chose to save the graphic in the last exercise because you are asked to present your graphics. You could have chosen to copy your graphic and then paste the graphic into another application. However, because you need to work with the graphics you find, it is better to save them to use later.

Key term

Context menu

A menu which is based on what the user is doing at the time. A graphics context menu is a menu specifically for working with graphics.

Sourcing graphics from clipart

You will probably already have used clipart. If you have, you will know that it is available in huge libraries of images. Many software applications include clipart libraries. In this way, you could think of clipart as a free resource which comes with other software.

As well as coming as a sort of free gift with software, clipart can be bought on its own. It can be downloaded from the Web or copied from a CD-ROM.

For this part of Unit 3, you need to include clipart from one of these two sources. It does not matter which, as long as the graphics you choose are relevant. If you read computer magazines, you will probably already have at least one CD-ROM containing clipart. If not, you will probably want to find graphics in an online clipart library. Websites such as **Clipart connection** (www.clipartconnection.com) contain huge amounts of clipart through which you can browse or which are presented to you once you have used criteria to search for them.

TIP

Criteria are the rules you set for a search. For example, if you wanted to find graphics for a publication about French cuisine, you would probably start by using two criteria – France and Cooking.

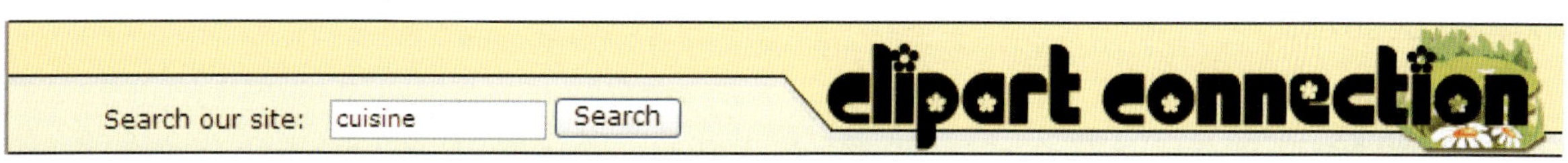

Figure 3.2: *Using a criterion to find graphics in an online clipart gallery.*

You may find that some of the graphics require payment before you can use them, but you will also find many which are available for use without charge. You will also find that many, especially photographs, will have a copyright acknowledgement on them. If you do use any clipart from these sites, you should not remove this acknowledgement.

Activity 2: Using an online clipart gallery...

In this activity you will:

- use a search engine to find a web-based clipart gallery
- search the clipart gallery for graphics for a publication about **Comedy**.

➔ Open your web browser and choose your favourite search engine.

➔ Use the criterion 'clipart galleries' to find a list of online clipart galleries.

➔ Choose a gallery. You can use any method you want to decide which gallery to pick – perhaps the name itself may be the best indication.

Your gallery will either give you a search facility or be organised into sections. Use any criteria you wish to find suitable graphics.

Key term

Clipart library

A collection of clipart. A clipart library may be included with other software or found on its own either on a CD-ROM or online.

Using a digital camera

If this book had been written a few years ago, this section would have started off with a paragraph explaining that although some mobile phones did have a camera attached, they were not of high enough quality to be used for assignments such as this one. However, camera phone technology has improved, so as long as you meet the requirements explained below then they are perfectly acceptable today.

The specification for the unit states that for any graphics captured using a digital camera, you must be able to:

- select image quality
- save graphics
- transfer graphics to a computer
- output graphics to a specific size.

You must meet these criteria for any graphics you take with a digital camera.

Select image quality

Different digital cameras will have different options for selecting image quality and you should either check the camera itself or its manual to find out which settings you can change. Many cameras allow you to change the size of the image as well as the resolution.

Saving graphics

If you are working on this unit at home, you will probably have a great deal of control over what you can do with your computer. This means that you will probably be able to connect your camera to your computer and transfer any photographs as you wish.

However, if you are not working at home, you will probably be working on a computer with restrictions on what you can do. In this case, you may need technical help to transfer any photographs from your camera to your work area.

There are two main ways in which you can transfer any photographs you take from a camera to a computer. As with selecting image quality, the options available for each individual camera will depend on the camera itself.

- Many cameras now come with a cable which connects either to a USB port or to a **Firewire** connector on your computer. Firewire usually achieves a faster data transfer rate than a USB connection. If you use a wire to physically connect your digital camera to your computer, your computer will probably detect that your camera has been attached and will automatically open the software you use to transfer photographs (often this is the software which was supplied with the camera). You should refer to your camera manual if you are not sure how to transfer your photographs.

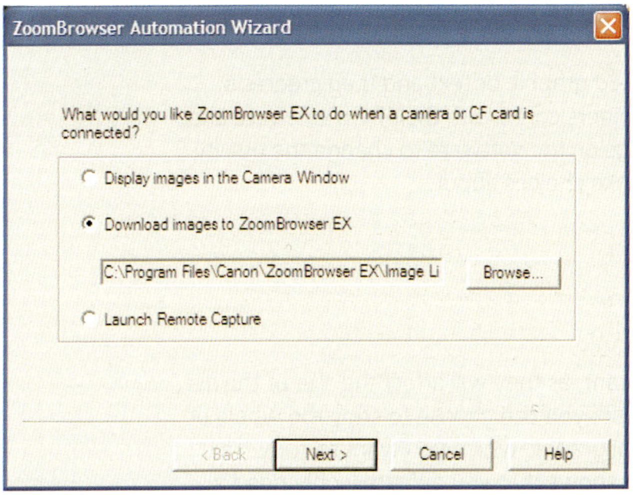

Figure 3.3: *Using software to transfer photographs from a digital camera to a computer.*

- Storage media are the items on to which any files are saved. Some cameras have removable storage media, which are usually called **storage cards**. These can hold a huge amount of data and can be removed from the camera and inserted into card readers which are either attached to your computer or actually built into your computer. Your computer will treat the card as a new **drive** when the card is inserted into the reader. You can then transfer the photograph files using Windows Explorer. Some digital cameras also have wireless transfer technology whereby the files are transferred via a shortwave radio signal using Bluetooth technology. Once you have found your photographs, you can then use the **Edit** → **Select All** followed by **Edit** → **Copy** to copy all of the photographs. Use **Edit** → **Paste** to paste them into your Unit 3 folder/directory.

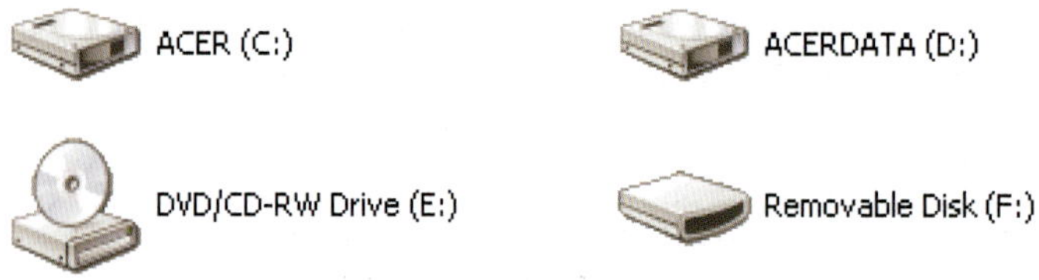

Figure 3.4: *Drives on a computer – Drive F is the removable drive.*

Key term

Storage media

The items to which any files are saved.

Digital camera photographs tend to be huge! Depending on your brief, you will probably need to resize them to suit the needs of your client. We will be looking at how to adjust the size of graphics in Chapter 5.

Using a scanner

A scanner is an input device that scans a paper-based graphic or text and then creates a digital copy which can be used on a computer. Scanners come with their own software and, just like digital cameras, you can change the settings on the software to change the quality of the graphic you create. For example, you can make choices about:

- the graphic type
- the graphic size and area
- the graphic resolution
- the colours used in the graphic.

As you have seen, each of these decisions is important, as they will affect the size of the file and what you can do with it. When you come to scan, you can choose to copy the whole of the original or you can select the part of the original graphic which you want to copy. This will save you work later, especially if your planning shows that you definitely only need a small part of a graphic. Choosing to only scan a part of a graphic will also free up storage space, because you will only be storing what you need, rather than a far larger file that you will edit later.

You also need to be careful about setting the resolution of your scan. We discussed resolution in Chapter 2, so you should understand that you need to scan the graphic at the resolution which suits your needs and plans.

Finally, many scanners will allow you to choose whether the scan is in colour or black and white. Make sure that your choice fits your plans!

Activity 3: Using images to suit a brief...

In this activity you will take and scan photographs to suit a brief.

Les and Des have always been proud of their relationship with their fans and want to build this into their tour posters. They have asked for a range of photographs of real people so that they can choose the best. These photographs will then have effects applied to them before they are used to create the final posters.

You have been asked to scan five photographs and take originals. You have been set the following brief:

- A total of five scanned and original photographs.
- A range of ages.
- At least one group of people.
- At least one person on their own.
- At least one 'head and shoulders' shot.
- At least one 'whole body' shot.
- All graphics should suit the family entertainment target audience.
- All graphics should show people who are happy or obviously enjoying themselves.
- The final poster will be A3 sized. The photographs or scans of people will cover approximately 33% of the poster.

You have been told that you should use both a digital camera and a scanner to capture these graphics.

- Plan the photographs and scans you are going to capture.
- Save all photographs and scans to your Unit 3 folder/directory.

Appropriate graphics

One last thing you must keep in mind is that you cannot just go off and find any graphics and put them into a display. Your graphics must be **appropriate**. This means that your graphics must suit the target audience and the actual task involved. If you look back at Activity 1 in this chapter, you were asked to find pictures of countryside from the North of England, so the graphics you find need to be appropriate. This means that the graphics should be countryside shots because city shots would not fit the brief and, in order to suit the target audience, must not include any offensive material. If, for example, you wanted a range of gently rolling hills and the best you could find were of hills in Ireland, then this is more acceptable and appropriate than if your gently rolling hills include herds of migrating wildebeest and the picture is clearly taken in Africa. Similarly, if your photograph of gently rolling hills was clearly of Yorkshire, but happened to be taken in a nudist colony, that would be inappropriate.

CHAPTER 4

Assessment Objective 4

Record the Sources of Computer Graphics and Consider Relevant Legislation

Overview:

This unit will explain how you should record where you found the graphics you collected in your work for Assessment Objective 3. You are strongly advised to complete this record, in full, as you complete this research.

How this assessment objective will be assessed...

You will be assessed on the following aspects of your work:

- The detail you include about where you found the graphics.
- The awareness you show of copyright law.

Skills to use...

You will need to:

- be organised
- record the full details (date of collection, file name, where found and size) of every graphic you find, whether it is a complete graphic or a part of a graphic
- remember that if you have done this task correctly, anyone should be able to find the graphic you have chosen simply by following your directions.

How to achieve...

Pass requirements

P1 You will use a table to keep a record of computer graphics sourced and stored.

Merit requirements

M1 You will use a table to keep a detailed record of computer graphics sourced and stored.

M2 Your record will include sufficient detail to allow others to locate some of the resources if they wished.

M3 You will show awareness of copyright law.

Distinction requirements

D1 You will use a table to keep an accurate record of computer graphics sourced and stored.

D2 Your record will include sufficient detail to allow others to locate most of the resources if they wished.

D3 You should have an awareness of copyright law.

Keeping records of the graphics you source

This is a straightforward process and, if you do it as you go along, you should achieve this assessment objective with little difficulty. Planning is the key to success here. Plan the table you are going to use to record all the necessary details before you start. Use it for your very first graphic and all that follow. Remember that these records should give full details, including location/source, so that someone else who wants to look at your graphics can find them.

The detail

The detail you store will depend on the source of the graphic you find. However, in general, you should include the following:

- the location/source
- the date of collection
- the filename
- the file size.

Providing the information

The information about the graphics you use needs to be presented in a table. A blank table you could use for this is shown below.

Graphic reference	Location/source of the graphic	Date of collection	Filename	File size	Copyright conditions

It is very important that you fill in the records as you find your graphics.

The first column has been provided so that you can refer to individual graphics with a clear reference. There are a number of ways you could refer to each graphic, for example you could use a description of the graphic, such as 'photograph with blue ribbon', or a number. Your descriptions should be clear and numbers should be clearly associated with the graphic. A printout of each graphic showing what it is called makes it clear which graphic is which.

There are other references you could use. You could, for example, use a name based on where the graphic is stored and the filename:

Mydocs\unit3\graphics\image1.jpg

However, this example table also asks for a location and this form of reference duplicates it without giving you much idea of what the graphic shows.

Alternatively, you could use a name based on when you collected the graphic. This would not be as potentially confusing as using the filename twice.

The location/source of each graphic

For many of your graphics, the location will be where in your folders you have saved the work. However, it is also worth including the source of your graphics. We will discuss each possible source of graphics in turn.

Resources found on the Web

For graphics found on the Web, the source is the information you need to provide so that somebody else can find the graphic. In order to find graphics on a website, you need to give the URL of the web page on which the graphic was found (this is the www address). However, you should also give some indication of where on the web page the graphic is located, especially if you are dealing with a web page which includes a lot of graphics. Even if the web page does not include a lot of graphics, giving the location of a graphic on a page is an example of good practice and is something you should do. A simple statement, saying that the graphic was at the top of the page on the left-hand side, would give sufficient information for most people to find a graphic.

However, for other graphics, things are not quite as simple. For clipart libraries, you would need to give the URL of the clipart gallery you used and any criteria or tabs you used to find the resources you have used.

TIP

Remember! You need to provide sufficient information about the source of a graphic so that someone else could find the same graphic.

Resources from a digital camera

Referencing a graphic collected with a digital camera is slightly more complicated, as you are basically referencing a photograph you have taken. If you are using a digital camera to capture graphics, the location of the photograph is probably sufficient. This could simply be an address, or maybe a description, such as 'at the end of the pier, Weston-super-Mare'.

Scanned resources

Any scanned resources you use will be graphics that have been digitised from an original graphic. These original graphics may be graphics you have created yourself or they may be graphics you have found elsewhere, perhaps in a magazine. If the graphic you are scanning is one which you have created yourself, then say so. You should keep the original graphic for reference.

If the graphic you wish to scan is from a magazine or other publication, you should include in your reference where the graphic was found. For a book, this reference must include:

- the name of the author
- the name of the photographer (if different from the author)
- the year the book was published
- the title of the book
- the publisher of the book
- the year of publication
- the page number where the graphic can be found.

For example, there are some graphics in the *Units 2 and 20* book of this series. If you chose to scan the storyboard example on page 112 of this book, your reference would be:

Graham Manson; 2007; Unit 2 Web page creation; Creating animation for the WWW using ICT; Page 112; Payne-Gallway, Oxford.

For a magazine or regular publication, your reference needs to include all of the above, as well as an indication of which month or period the publication covers – for example, you may state that the graphic was originally included in the July 2007 issue of a magazine.

Date of collection

This is simply a case of giving the date on which you got the graphic. This should be the full date, including the year.

Filename

As mentioned above, you need to provide the filename for each graphic. If you collect graphics from the Web, you may be tempted to use the filename used by the person who created the website. However, this may not be as clear and meaningful for your purposes as you would hope. The screenshot below shows a graphic about to be saved from a website.

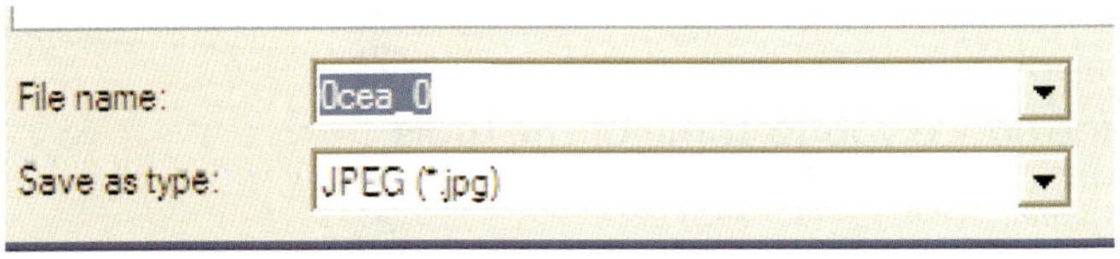

Figure 4.1: *Saving a graphic file downloaded from the Web.*

File size

We discussed **file size** in Chapter 1 of this unit. If you need to, you should go back and refresh your memory now.

Copyright law

The final stage of this process is to be aware of whether or not you need to ask permission before you use any graphics you find. The specifications for this unit are clear that you do not need to actually ask for permission to use graphics, just be aware of whether you should.

Resources from the Web

In general, any materials placed on the Internet are covered by copyright law. This means that any graphics or pieces of text you place on the Internet remain your property. Anyone who uses your materials has to ask for permission before they do so.

There are, however, some exceptions to this law. The most important as far as you are concerned applies to the use of materials for what is called 'non-commercial use and private study'. This exception means that as long as you are using the graphics for private study or an educational course, you are allowed to use the graphics, but your work must include sufficient acknowledgement. If you use work that is covered by copyright, a simple reference to the copyright holder is sufficient. In your notes for the graphic, you should then explain that you would usually need permission to use such a graphic, but as your work is for an educational purpose, you do not need to request such permission.

Other resources

Graphics scanned from a magazine or other source are covered by the same copyright rules as graphics sourced from the Web.

Finally, any graphics you create, and so did not exist before, are yours. These include digital photographs you have taken. You hold the copyright for these graphics and do not have to apply. In fact, if anyone in your class wanted to use these graphics for purposes other than educational, they would actually need to check with you for permission.

TIP

Further information on copyright can be found on the Intellectual Property Office website at http://www.ipo.gov.uk/copy.htm.

CHAPTER 5

Assessment Objective 5

Use Appropriate Software Tools to Create, Edit and Combine Graphic Images

Overview:

This Assessment Objective asks you to use appropriate tools to create, edit and combine graphic images. This chapter will introduce you to some of the tools included in Macromedia® Fireworks®.

In order to complete the activities in this chapter you will need access to a number of additional files. These files are contained in the Unit 3 Student Resources zip file which can be downloaded from the OCR Nationals in ICT (Units 3 & 5) Student Resources page on the Payne-Gallway website: www.payne-gallway.co.uk

How this assessment objective will be assessed...

You will be assessed on the following aspects of your work:

- The range of tools you use.
- The evidence you provide that shows you have developed graphics.
- Your ability to save graphics in an appropriate format.

Skills to use...

This chapter looks at the use of a wide range of graphics tools. Fireworks® groups these into **Bitmap** and **Vector** tools. However, all tools included in the software may be combined to create exciting and effective graphics, so this chapter groups the tools into those that are used to create graphics, those that work with objects and those that work with whole graphics.

You need to use as wide a range of tools and effects as you can. Fireworks® has a huge range of tools and there is not enough space to discuss them all here. We have concentrated on those listed in the specification. As you work with Fireworks® through the activities in this chapter, you may notice tools that have not been mentioned. Do not ignore them because these can be as effective as those that have been explained and will be rewarded as readily.

How to achieve...

Pass requirements

P1 You will create graphics using a limited range of vector and bitmap tools.

P2 You will provide some evidence that you have developed graphics.

Merit requirements

M1 You will use a range of vector and bitmap tools to create graphics that are fit for purpose.

M2 You will provide evidence that you have developed graphics. This evidence will be annotated to explain the processes undertaken.

M3 Most of the graphics you produce will be saved in appropriate formats.

Distinction requirements

D1 You will use a wide range of vector and bitmap tools to create graphics that are fit for purpose.

D2 You will provide evidence that you have developed graphics. This evidence will be annotated to explain and justify the processes undertaken.

D3 All of the graphics you produce will be saved in appropriate formats.

The project

Les and Des need a range of graphics to use on their website. You will create some of these as you work through the chapter. You will be given other graphics to create at the end of the chapter. The graphics you need to create will be based on the wide range of tools and effects explained below. The activities in this chapter have been designed so that you can learn and practise the skills you need to carry out the project for your clients. In the final activity you will use your new-found skills and complete the various graphic elements required by your clients: Les and Des.

General comments

Showing development

As you work through your project, you will be developing graphics. As you do so, you will need to create evidence to show you have developed your ideas. This is often something that students ignore until it is too late. However, if you are well organised and regularly save your work at different stages of production, you will soon build up a portfolio of evidence. This evidence may include graphics you did not use or graphics that changed a great deal before they were finished. If you intend to edit a graphic, the original version, as well as proof of editing, will be evidence that you have developed your work.

Saving files in appropriate formats

Fireworks® saves files by default in .png format. However, when you complete your graphics, you may **export** them in a suitable format using the **Optimize** panel. The **Optimize** options allow you to save your work as GIFs (.gif – including animated GIFs) or JPEGs (.jpg). You are creating graphics to use on the Web, so either of these formats are suitable.

Bitmap and vector graphics

The two differences between bitmap and vector graphics were discussed in Chapter 1. You should look there again to remind yourself of the features of these graphic types.

Macromedia® Fireworks®

When you open Fireworks® you will be asked whether you want to create a new file or open an existing one. Fireworks® can be used to work with a wide range of graphics types, so you should be able to open just about any graphic you have.

If you decide to create a new graphic, you will need to complete the **New Document** dialogue box (Figure 2.1). You need to give the dimensions of your new graphic in **Pixels**, **Inches** or **Centimetres**. 'Inches' and 'centimetres' are self-explanatory. 'Pixels' refers to each dot on the screen.

As well as the size of the graphic, you are asked to decide on the resolution of the graphic. The default setting is 72 Pixels/Inch (which means 72 dots per inch or 72 dpi) and this is sufficient for most work you will be doing. Just remember that the higher the resolution, the more detail the graphic holds and so the bigger the file size.

You also need to decide on the colour of the canvas. This is the background colour of the graphic you are about to create.

Once you have either created a new graphic or opened an existing one, you will be faced with what can be a very confusing layout. Along the top of the screen is a menu which gives the usual drop-down lists of commands such as **Open**, **Save**, etc. On the left-hand side of the screen, there is a toolbar. You will be looking at this toolbar in more detail as you work through this chapter.

On the right of the screen, there is a range of grouped options and tools sheets. These are called **Panels** and can be opened or closed as you wish. When you first start using the software, it is probably better to close any that are open by clicking on the arrowhead just to the left of the title of the panel.

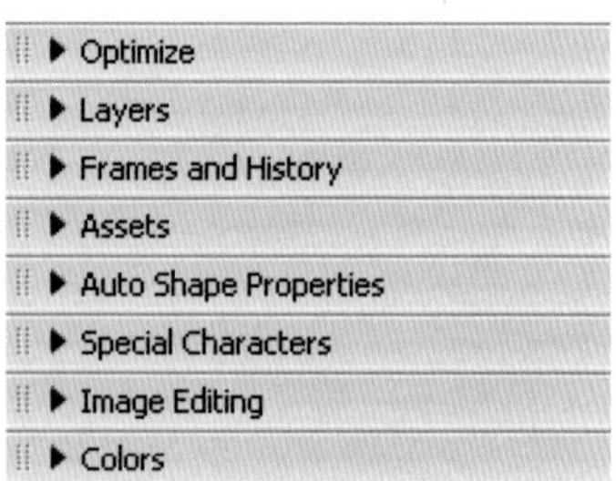

Figure 5.1: *The Fireworks® panels.*

The **Properties** panel is at the bottom of the Fireworks® screen. This panel is extremely useful as it brings together all the properties and settings for the currently selected item. This can include information about size, colour and type.

There is an area at the bottom left of the Properties panel that can be used to name any objects you create. It is a good idea to name any objects you create, especially in more complicated graphics that include many objects, as this will allow you to keep track of all elements in a graphic.

As you work with the different tools, keep an eye on this panel. It will change depending on what you are doing with the software. You will soon learn that the Properties panel is one of the most useful features included with the package.

Fireworks® tools

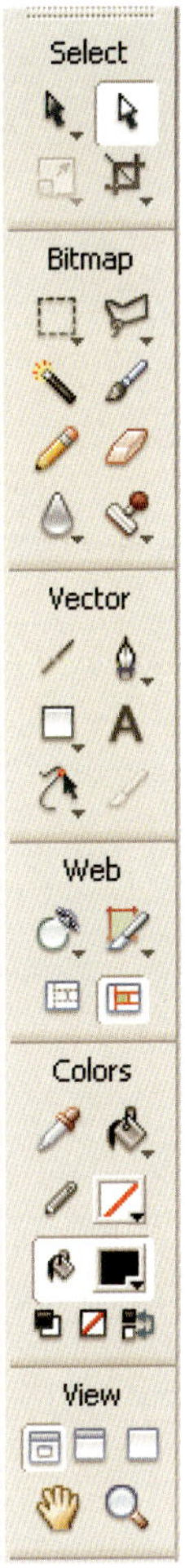

Figure 5.2: *The Fireworks® toolbar.*

Macromedia® Fireworks® includes tools which you would normally find in a vector graphics package, as well as tools you would usually find in a bitmap graphics package.

As you would expect, Fireworks® offers you a wide range of tools that you can use to create and edit graphics. These are organised into five main editing groups, with a sixth group which contains the tools you will use to view the graphics you have created. The editing groups are:

- Select
- Bitmap
- Vector
- Web
- Colors

Each of these groups contains a number of icons, not all of which are directly visible. You would be forgiven, for example, for assuming that there are four tools within the **Select** group. However, you would be wrong. There are, in fact, eight tools. This is because any icon which includes a small down arrow at the bottom right is actually part of a sub-menu. This sub-menu can be accessed by clicking on the tool icon and holding down the left-hand mouse button.

The screenshot shows the sub-menu with which the **Pointer tool** is associated.

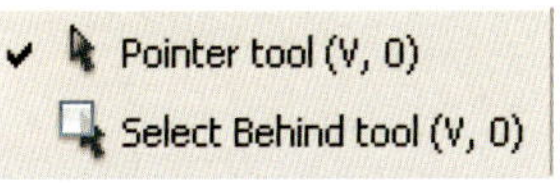

Figure 5.3: *The sub-menu with which the Pointer tool is associated.*

As you will have noticed, two of the groups are called **Bitmap** and **Vector**. Tools in the **Bitmap** group are those which allow you to work with pixels to create graphics. Those in the **Vector** group allow you to create graphics by creating and combining shapes.

Tools in the **Select** group are similar to those you may have come across in other graphics software packages. These tools include ones to point, select and crop.

Tools in the **Web** group are possibly the most exciting of all the tools which are included with Fireworks® by letting you create web graphics. Many of the tools included in this group, such as the **Hotspot** tool, are tools which were once considered to be specialist web design tools only a few years ago. These tools allow you to add web-ready effects to graphics, so that, for example, a graphic may be added straight onto a website with hotspots already created.

The **Colors** tools are those which deal with colour!

Unfortunately, there is not enough space to go through all the tools that Fireworks® includes. We will, however, concentrate on those tools which are specifically mentioned in the specification for the unit.

Select tools

There are four tools in the **Select** group. When you first open Fireworks®, these icons are:

- the Pointer tool
- the Subselection tool
- the Scale tool
- the Crop tool.

The specification requires that you include the use of selection tools in your work. While this set of tools does include other options, the four tools listed above could be considered to be the four most important ones and so we will concentrate on these.

The Pointer tool

The **Pointer tool** allows you to select an object by pointing and clicking. If you think of this as having the same function as your mouse pointer, you will have a good understanding of how this tool is used.

The Subselection tool

When you use the Pointer tool to select an object, the object appears with **anchor points**. Using the **Subselection tool**, these anchor points can be dragged to distort the graphic.

The Scale tool

The **Scale tool** allows you to resize any object by clicking on any of the eight anchor points around the outside of the graphic. This tool also includes a **rotation** tool which can be used to rotate a graphic by clicking anywhere **outside** the graphic and holding down the left mouse button while moving the mouse. By default, this part of the tool rotates the graphic around a central point. However, you can change the point around which the graphic rotates by moving the reference point which is in the centre of the graphic when you first select the tool.

The Crop tool

The **Crop tool** is a standard graphics package tool and allows you to remove any parts of a graphic that are not needed. For example, you might wish to crop a photograph which is great in every respect, except that as you took the photograph someone walked into the edge of the shot. Highlight the area of the graphic that you want to keep and then double click within the selection to remove the parts outside the selected area.

Key term

Anchor point

These are key points around the edge of a graphic. In Fireworks®, they include the four corners of a graphic, as well as one on each side. The Scale tool also uses an anchor point that appears in the centre of the graphic by default, but which may be moved.

Activity 1: Using the Crop tool...

In this activity you will use the Crop tool to remove unwanted parts of a picture.

You will be working on the graphic **Les and Des 1.jpg** in this activity.

As we know, things have been a bit difficult for Les and Des recently. To save money, the photographs for the forthcoming tour were taken in the dining room of a close friend.

Unfortunately, the photographer, another close friend, has managed to include pieces of furniture on the left- and right-hand sides of **Les and Des 1,** as well as a child's toy. Les and Des like the graphic, but do not want these objects included in the published version. They would like to remove the left- and the right-hand margins from the graphic.

- Open the graphic **Les and Des 1.jpg**.
- Use the Crop tool to select the middle of the graphic.
- Double click within the selected area to remove the rest of the graphic.

Drawing and painting techniques

As we discussed above, there are many tools included with Fireworks®. Many of these tools are used to change graphics. However, there are also many tools that are used to create graphics from scratch. **These tools are included in both the Bitmap and the Vector groups**. Rather than concentrate on tools by group, we will discuss tools by what they do. Therefore, this section will deal with those tools that are used to create graphics.

The view tools

Before we start looking at the range of tools included with Fireworks®, we need to mention the **View** menu. This is a very important menu, as it includes **Zoom In**, **Zoom Out** and **Magnification**. These three menu items can be used to change the view you have of the graphics on which you are working. **Zoom In** and **Zoom Out** allow you take gradual steps closer to or further from your graphic, respectively. **Magnification** lets you choose the magnification without taking the gradual steps of the zoom commands.

These are very important tools because you will need to zoom into your graphics so that you can do more accurate work.

TIP

Zooming does not change the size of the graphic. When you zoom in or zoom out, you are merely getting closer to or further away from a graphic, respectively.

Freehand tools

Freehand tools work as though you are using a pen or pencil. The mouse is used to control the location of the 'nib' and you are not provided with any guides to help you with the work.

The main Freehand tools are the **Pencil tool** and the **Brush tool** (both in the Bitmap group).

Brush type and shape

Fireworks® allows you to change how the Freehand tools appear by changing the style of brush or width of the pen stroke.

We have already mentioned the **Properties** panel and pointed out that this is one of the most useful features of Fireworks®. It is important to keep an eye on the Properties panel as you work through the different tools mentioned above to see how the panel changes to suit the tool with which you are working.

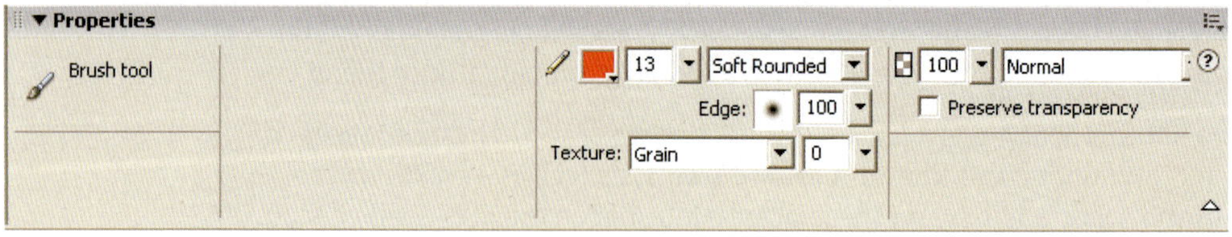

Figure 5.4: *The Properties panel for the Brush tool.*

Take a look at the **Properties panel** for the **Brush tool**. There are some interesting features. First, there is a handy little label on the left, just to remind you what tool you are using. On the right-hand side of the panel, there are a group of options that let you alter the quality, texture, size and colour of the brush stroke. These are excellent for choosing exactly what you want the brush stroke to look like when applied to the 'canvas'. Just because the tool is called a **Brush tool**, you should not assume you are just working with a brush. You can use this tool to select other drawing implements. Perhaps you want your work to look as if it has been created with an airbrush or a felt-tip pen. You may even decide you would rather use something 'unnatural', such as **Toxic Waste** or **Viscous Alien Paint** (whatever these are!). These are all options included in the **Stroke category** drop-down list.

The other useful options in this area are the **Tip size** option – the larger the number here, the bigger the tip size. Simple really! This option is common to many different tools and you can use it to change the size of the line or other object with which you are working, such as text. You can either type a number directly into this box or use the slider that appears when you click the down arrow to the right of the displayed number.

TIP

The slider tool only goes up to 96. However, you can enter far bigger numbers if you type in your own. Settings above 96, however, result in huge sizes!

Using colours and different fill styles

Colour and fill style are other attributes that can be changed in the **Properties panel**.

Colours are chosen by clicking on the colour option box (the coloured rectangle that appears on the **Properties panel** and in the **Color** tool group). This will bring up a palette of colours from which you can choose the one you wish to use. When you choose a colour, the cursor changes to a dropper. As your dropper moves over the colours, you are given a six-digit colour code in the top window. This is called the **hexadecimal** value for the colour. We will use these values when we are taking about colours. To find a specific colour, you can either select it from the palette or type the hexadecimal value, beginning with the #, into the text box above the palette.

When you come to work on a commission or a brief, you may be given a **Red Green Blue** (RGB) value for any colours you have been asked to use. This would usually be if a business wants you to use specific colours (for example, their corporate colours). If you are given the RGB values for colours, you can enter them in another colour palette which is displayed by clicking on the colour wheel icon at the top right of the hexadecimal palette.

If you click the down arrow to open the **Fill category** option (e.g. displayed in the **Paint bucket tool** Properties panel), you will be presented with six different options. The first of these is the option not to have a fill. However, the remaining options give you a wide range of fill styles.

- **Web dither**. This is extremely useful if you have been asked to use a specific colour for a graphic you are creating for a website. This may be the colour of a school's badge, for example. There are a wide range of colours that cannot be used on the Web and it is quite likely that the colour you need to create your graphic is one of those colours. The Web creates a pattern based on the two colours to create the illusion of the colour you need, but the detail of how this is done is beyond the scope of this book. If you are asked to use such a colour, a Web search using the criteria **web dither** will bring up plenty of helpful websites.
- **Solid** is exactly what it says. The colour fill is a solid block of colour.
- **Gradient**. You will probably have come across a gradient fill in other software packages. This is the fill that gradually swaps the main fill colour into white. There are many different gradient patterns from which to choose. Experiment and find one you like.
- **Pattern** provides you with a choice of many different patterns that your fill could take. Again you will need to experiment to see if there are any useful patterns in the graphics you produce.
- **Fill options**. This combines all of the fill options, including options such as **Edge** (e.g. whether the edge is a sharp cutoff or soft), the **Texture** of the fill (which gives you further options on how the fill appears) and the **Amount** of texture.

As well as all these options, you are given the chance to make the shape you are creating transparent. If you choose this option, your shape will be, to some extent, see-through.

TIP

Remember the audience and the task! When you are presented with such a wide range of tools from which to choose, it is often tempting to use as many as you can to create really shocking graphics. However, before you use these effects, ask yourself whether these effects will suit the audience or the client.

Lines

There are two tools in the **Vector** group that allow you to work with lines. The first is the **Line tool**. This works as you might expect and lets you create a straight line. As usual, the **Properties panel** can be used to change the setting for lines. The options for lines are basically the same as for the **Brush tool** (explained above).

The second tool is the **Freeform tool**. This tool is used to transform objects by clicking on any part of the object and dragging using the mouse until the object is sufficiently distorted. This tool can only be used to transform another object created using tools within the **Vector** group. This tool may be used to create curves in straight lines or can be used to distort a shape such as one of the shapes created in the next section.

Creating geometric and freehand shapes

This is an impressive title to hide something that is extremely straightforward. Fireworks® includes a wide range of preset shapes within the **Vector** group. You will need to display the menu list by clicking on the displayed shape tool and holding down the mouse button. These shapes range from simple rectangles and ellipses, through to L shapes, spiral and stars.

Each of these shapes is drawn in the same way. Activity 2 will explain this further.

Activity 2: Create a flag...

In this activity you will create a flag which has four stars in a line from top left to bottom right. (A version of the finished flag is shown in Figure 5.5.)

- Create a new Fireworks® graphic. This graphic needs to be 600 pixels wide and 400 pixels high. Set the resolution to 72 pixels per inch and the canvas colour to white.
- Select the shape tool from the **Vector** group. (By default, this will be set to **Rectangle tool**.)
- Select the **Star** shape.
- Click on the top left of the graphic, just in from the edge of the frame, and, holding down the left mouse button, drag towards the bottom right until you have drawn out a star that covers about 10% of the canvas.
- Move diagonally down across the page and repeat the steps above to create three more stars.
- Save your graphic as **Flag**. We will be using it again later.

Figure 5.5: *The finished flag from Activity 2.*

Activity 3: Use blocks of colour to produce a simple shape...

In this activity you will create a simple graphic based on blocks and circles.

Figure 5.6 has been created by combining blocks of colour. These blocks of colour have had different fill effects applied to them.

Figure 5.6: *A simple graphic created by combining shapes.*

Either attempt to recreate Figure 5.6 **or** design and create your own graphic using simple blocks of colour.

Working with text

The **Text tool** A is part of the **Vector** group of tools.

To add text to your graphic, click on the icon and then select where on the graphic you want your text to appear. As you type, the text box will expand. However, be warned that you need to use returns at the end of any line – the text tool does not 'wrap' the text for you. However, once you have finished entering your text, you can use the **Select** tools to reshape the text box and this will wrap your text for you.

Notice that the **Properties** panel includes many of the tools we have already discussed in the previous section on fill styles. As well as these, you will see some other icons included which you have probably seen before. Icons such as **Bold, Italic** and **Underline** should be old friends. There is also a font type selection area, as well as areas where you can manipulate the position of the text on the screen and the size of the text box.

Activity 4: Adding text to the flag...

In this activity you will add text to your **Flag** graphic.

Many flags have the name of the country or organisation they represent included on them. You are now going to add some text to the flag you created in Activity 3.

- Open your **Flag** graphic.
- Think of some text you want to enter onto your flag – this could be the name of a country or organisation, or maybe a motto.
- Using Batang font, colour #FF0000 and size 50, add your text at the bottom left of the flag.
- Save your graphic as **Flag and Text**.

Figure 5.7: *The stars flag with text.*

Using layers

The simplest way to think of layers is to imagine a graphic being made up of many clear plastic sheets, each with a separate part of the overall graphic printed on it. One sheet may have a piece of text and another may have a background. You can edit each layer but it is impossible to tell what the overall graphic is until all layers are combined.

One of the benefits of working with layers in a graphic is that different parts of the graphic are kept separate. As different layers can also be switched on and off, you are able to hide any layers that you do not need to edit or to guide you, and then concentrate on those layers which you need. In the exercise you have just completed, you created two separate object groups on one layer. These were the stars group and the text group. If you were to continue working with this graphic, you would find that as you add more information to the graphic it becomes complicated to work on. If you add each new element as a new layer, these layers can be switched on or off to make your work easier.

Creating layers

New layers are created in the **Layers** panel. This lets you see all layers included in the graphic. Here you can switch layers on and off and, using the layers option menu, merge layers so that they are all combined into one bitmap layer.

The **Layers** panel should be at the top right of the screen. If you can see the title but no details, you need to open it by clicking on the arrowhead which is pointing to the right, towards the title of the panel.

The four main tools on this panel are at the bottom of the panel and include the tools to create a new layer or sub-layer. However, to the right of the panel title is an icon that opens the **Options** drop-down menu. This menu includes the same four main tools, as well as many more. The **Thumbnail Options...** tool is extremely useful as it allows you to change the size of the thumbnails that appear in the panel. This is especially useful if you include many objects and layers in your work or if you have difficulty seeing thumbnails that are too small.

***Figure 5.8:** The Layers panel Options drop-down menu.*

Selecting, moving and positioning layers

As you create more complicated graphics, so the number of layers you include in your graphic will increase. If you wish to go back to work on a layer you have already created, this is simply a case of clicking on the layer within the stack in order to select it.

The **Layers** panel shows layers in the order they were created. The newest layers are at the top of the list and the oldest are at the bottom. The newer layers are also nearer to the front of the graphic and obscure what happens behind. This is fine if you create layers in a logical order, but if you forget to add something to the background and have to add the layer later, this may hide objects you wanted to be in the front of the graphic. Imagine spending ages working on a picture of a cute rabbit but hiding it with a picture of a mountain! The next activity explains what to do if a similar potential disaster happens to your work.

Activity 5: Working with layers...

In this activity you will create a multilayered graphic.

There's been a revolution and you need to change the flag! The 'Spirals' have taken over. Luckily, Fireworks® includes a spiral. Open your **Flag and Text** graphic.

- Create a new layer. It will appear in the panel as Layer 2. Double click on this layer and rename it **Spiral**.
- Select the **Shape** tool and choose the **Spiral**.
- Add a spiral at the bottom left of the flag. This will overlap the text you have already added.
- Select the #996666 fill colour to add a colour fill to the spiral you have just added. Your spiral will now partially hide the text you have already added.

If you now look at the layers in the **Layers** panel, you will see that you have two layers. The new layer, the one called **Spiral**, is at the top of the list. The order is important as the higher up the list a layer is, the nearer to the front of the picture is the content of the layer. The spiral layer is hiding the text in Layer 1 because Layer 1 is behind the Spiral layer.

- Click on the name of the Spiral layer with the left mouse button and, keeping your finger on the left mouse button, drag the spiral layer to the bottom of the pile.

Your flag should now show the spiral emblem behind the text.

- Save your file as **Spiral flag**.

Figure 5.9: *The spiral flag with text.*

When we first discussed layers, we mentioned that the best way to think of them is as elements on separate pieces of clear plastic sheets. Think of this because it helps to explain the final thing about layers. When you move one element of a layer, you can, by choice, move them all. In the above task, because the text and the stars are on the same layer, you can select the layer from the layer stack within the **Layers** panel and move the whole of the layer. This means that all the elements on the layer stay in the same relative position to each other and all move to a new location relative to other layers.

If you do want to move one element on a layer, this can be done by either clicking on the individual object on the graphic or on the layer stack.

Filters

Filters are specialised tools within a graphics package. They perform standard tasks, such as applying a distortion. Filters can be applied to whole graphics or elements of graphics.

Fireworks® does not include a large number of filters, but those it does have can be used to good effect.

Like many other Fireworks® tools, filters are best applied from the **Properties panel**. In the next activity, you will look at using a filter to distort a graphic so that it looks like a button.

Activity 6: Create a button...

In this activity you will create a button.

- Choose **File** → **New** to create a new file. This file needs to be 125 pixels wide and 75 pixels high.
- Now use the rectangle tool to create a rectangle which is 125 pixels wide and 75 pixels high. You should have a go at drawing this freehand, but if you are not totally accurate, you can make any necessary changes to the rectangle by changing the settings for the rectangle in the **Properties panel**.

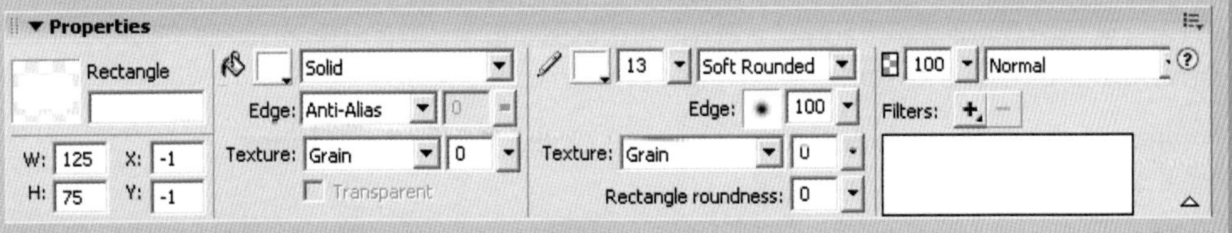

***Figure 5.10:** The properties of the rectangular shape.*

- Now fill the rectangle you have created with a solid colour fill. This is done by choosing the **Paint Bucket** tool. Once you have done this, press the **Escape** key on the keyboard and then choose the **Select** tool.
- With the rectangle selected, look to the right of the **Properties panel**. There is an area labelled **Filters**. Click on the **+** sign to bring up the list of available effects. Choose **Bevel and Emboss** → **Inner Bevel**.

You should now see that your rectangle looks more like a button.

The **Inner Bevel** filter can also be used to create sections within a graphic to look as though they are three dimensional.

Activity 7: Using filters...

In this activity you will use the **Bevel and Emboss** filter to create three-dimensional elements within a graphic.

You have presented the Spiral flag as an example of your work to your clients, Les and Des, and they have asked you to make it look a bit more impressive. They would like you to include a three dimensional graphic. Follow the steps below to make the stars and the spiral appear as though they are three dimensional.

- Open the **Spiral flag** graphic.
- Select one of the stars on the flag.
- Apply the **Inner Bevel** filter to this star to make it appear three dimensional.
- Repeat for all remaining stars and the spiral.
- Save your file as **Improved spiral**.

You may have used similar filters in other software packages, but it is worth spending some time researching the filters that are included with Fireworks®, for example there is an excellent **Motion Blur** that you can use to make a graphic look as though the object is moving.

Another filter you may want to use is the **Shadow and Glow** filter. This gives you five options. These are:

- Drop Shadow
- Glow
- Inner Glow
- Inner Shadow
- Solid Shadow

The **Drop Shadow** option creates a shadow behind the graphic. When you create a shadow using this filter, you can set the size of the shadow, and the distance and angle it makes from the original. An angle of 0° is to the right and an angle of 90° is directly up.

The **Glow** option creates a coloured highlighted area around an object, whereas the **Inner Glow** option creates a similar effect inside the shape.

Some of these filters also give you a **Knock out** option. This makes it look as if the original image has been removed, but the shadow left.

Figure 5.11: *The Drop Shadow filter (with and without Knock out) and the Glow filter.*

Working with elements

Grouping

This section will look at how you can work with elements which appear in your graphics. We have already discussed how you can use the layers to move elements on the same layer around a graphic, but you now need to consider how you would group separate elements together to create a new element. These could be elements in a picture of a flower or a car, for example.

Grouping is the process of combining together individual elements into one new whole. When used in graphics, grouping joins together separate elements so that these separate elements now always appear together as part of a new graphic.

Activity 8: Grouping objects...

In this activity you will create a grouped graphic.

Figure 5.12 is made up of a number of different shapes, mostly ellipses. These have been grouped so that the graphic is now one single object.

- Create a new graphic using drawing tools. (You could use just **Vector** or just **Bitmap** tools to create your graphic or you could combine tools from both groups.)
- Select all the objects in your graphic by holding the **Shift** key down while clicking each object.
- Group your objects by choosing **Modify** → **Group**.

Your graphic will now be grouped into one new object.

Figure 5.12: *A grouped graphic.*

TIP

Another method of selecting all objects in a graphic is to choose the Select tool and then, with the left mouse button held down, drag your cursor to cover the graphic. As you do so, a box will appear. Drag the box to surround all objects and this will select all objects within the box.

As well as **grouping** an object, you can **ungroup** (**Modify** → **Ungroup**). This is the process of breaking a graphic into the separate objects that were used to create it. This is extremely useful if you want to change one object within a graphic. You may, for example, decide that the penguin, in the example, could be improved by adding a yellow stomach. This would be best achieved by working on the ellipse that was used to create the white area that is the stomach. You could not do this unless all the objects in the graphic were ungrouped.

Order and alignment

We have already discussed the use of the **Layers** panel to change the **order** in which graphics appear. The order of the layers can also be changed using **Modify** → **Arrange**. It has exactly the same effect as clicking on the object and either dragging it further up the stack (which is called **Bring Forward**), dragging it to the top of the stack (**Bring to Front**), dragging it further down the stack (**Send Backward**) or dragging it to the bottom of the stack (**Send to Back**).

Bring to Front	Ctrl+Shift+UP
Bring Forward	Ctrl+UP
Send Backward	Ctrl+DOWN
Send to Back	Ctrl+Shift+DOWN

Figure 5.13: *The Arrange options*

Finally in this section, we come to **alignment**. Sometimes when working with graphics, we want to align elements around a common point. We might, for example, want all elements to be aligned along one common central point, or so that the left-hand sides of each graphic are in a straight line.

This can be a very difficult process to do by eye. However, use **Modify** → **Align** to let Fireworks® align selected objects.

Left	Ctrl+Alt+1
Center Vertical	Ctrl+Alt+2
Right	Ctrl+Alt+3
Top	Ctrl+Alt+4
Center Horizontal	Ctrl+Alt+5
Bottom	Ctrl+Alt+6
Distribute Widths	Ctrl+Alt+7
Distribute Heights	Ctrl+Alt+9

Figure 5.14: *The Align options.*

The first six align options are all straightforward and can be used to line up objects as described. The final two options allow you to evenly distribute the heights or widths of three or more selected objects.

Working with graphics

The previous two sections dealt with those tools that we use to create graphics. This section deals with those tools which are more to do with editing the graphics you create or collect.

Cut, copy, crop and paste

We have already discussed the **Crop** tool. As you found out, this tool is used to remove those parts around the edge of a graphic that you no longer need. We will now discuss the **Cut**, **Copy** and **Paste** tools.

You may have used the cut, copy and paste tools in other software packages. However, because Fireworks® works with objects and selections, these processes are slightly more complicated. We will start by thinking about what you do if you are working with an object.

- To **cut** an object, you simply select it with the selection tool and choose **Edit** → **Cut**.
- To **copy** an object, choose **Edit** → **Copy**.
- To **paste** an object, such as one you have previously cut or copied, simply choose **Edit** → **Paste**.

These are pretty straightforward. We will now look at working with these tools with areas within a graphic. There are three main uses here. The first is to copy an area of one graphic and paste it onto another. The second is to copy an element and paste an exact copy (a clone). The third is to replace one area with material from another area on the same graphic.

We will look at each in order. However, before we do, we need to have a quick look at the tools used to select areas of a graphic. The tools for doing this are:

- the **Marquee** tool. This is used to select a rectangular area of the graphic.
- the **Oval** marquee tool (hold down the marquee tool). This is used to select an elliptical area.
- The **Lasso** tool is used to select an irregular area of the graphic.
- The **Polygon Lasso** tool is used to select an irregular straight-edged area of the graphic.
- The **Magic Wand** tool is used to select areas of similar coloured pixels.

Copy from one graphic and paste onto another

This is the traditional copy and paste task you will have probably used before. This takes an area of one graphic and then pastes it onto another. The next Activity explores this technique.

Activity 9: Copying and pasting...

In this activity you will copy one area of a graphic and paste it onto another.

Les and Des would like a graphic made up of many copies of their heads. This will be placed at the bottom of their tour poster. They would like you to use the heads on all the **Les and Des** graphics, which are available in the Unit 3 Student Resources zip file. We will start by copying the first pair of heads.

- Create a new Fireworks® file. The dimensions should be 5 cm high and 21 cm wide. We will use a white background. Save this graphic as **Heads**.
- Open the file **Les and Des 1.jpg**.
- Use the **Lasso** tool to select the heads of Les and Des. Choose **Edit** → **Copy** to make a copy of the two heads.
- Open the new Heads graphic you have created.
- Choose **Edit** → **Paste** to paste the copied heads onto the graphic.
- Create a new layer.
- Repeat with all the graphics that Les and Des have supplied you.

As you paste new heads into the document, you will need to use the **Select** tool to move the selections around. Try to get an even distribution of heads on the page. You should also work with the **Order** tool so that the heads can be seen. Les has asked that his head (**Les and Des 21**) should be used as the central face on the graphic.

- You should export your completed graphic as **JPEG – Better Quality**.

Cloning

All those fans of science fiction or maybe even science fact will know that **cloning** is the process of making an exact copy of something. This is exactly the same when used in graphics. Cloning is used to make a copy of a selected area of a graphic. This copy can then be pasted back onto the original graphic. The cloned area is pasted back over exactly the same area as was copied, from where it can be selected and dragged to where it needs to appear on the graphic.

The Rubber Stamp tool

This is an excellent tool for replacing one part of a graphic with another. This could be used to remove a blemish on a photograph or a small detail that is not required. Maybe you even want to change a photograph to pretend that someone was not there! This tool takes one part of a graphic and allows you to copy this into a selected area of pixels.

Once you have selected your pixels, you can use the **Rubber Stamp** tool to select the area of the graphic you wish to 'paint' onto the graphic. This tool works by setting an area of a graphic that you are going to use to paint over another area. It is best to work with small areas at a time when using this tool. Relax, it is far harder to explain than it is to do and the results are excellent!

Activity 10 looks at this further. You will be using the file **fire.jpg**. We want to replace the area of tent behind the fire with grass. We will use the area of grass at the bottom left-hand side of the graphic as the source for this.

Activity 10: Using the Rubber Stamp tool...

In this activity you will use the **Rubber Stamp** tool to improve a graphic by removing a problem area.

- Open the file **fire.jpg**, which can be found in the Unit 3 Student Resources zip file.
- Use the **Lasso** tool to select a small area at the top left of the graphic. This is the area into which we will be painting. We use the **Lasso** tool because the human eye notices irregular areas far less readily than it notices areas made up of straight lines.
- Choose the **Rubber Stamp** tool. A target icon will appear. It is important that you choose your area correctly, because this selects the source area from which you are painting. Choose an area of grass at the bottom left of the graphic.
- Once you have selected your source area, your cursor will become a blue circle. Use your mouse to move this blue circle to the area of the white canvas you want to replace.
- Hold down the left mouse button and move the circle around the selected area. As you do so, the pixels from the source area will replace those over which you are drawing. Also, the blue cross will move to show you the area from which you are copying. Do not worry if you stray into the area of the fire or the metal container, you can overwrite them with another selection.
- Once you have filled your selection, use the **Lasso** tool to select a new area and then reselect your source area with the **Rubber Stamp** tool. Fill your new area.

This is best done in a series of small steps. As you near the end, you might find it useful to zoom in to get more accuracy.

As you practise with the **Rubber Stamp** tool, you will find that you become increasingly accurate. You will also find that quite dramatic effects can be achieved quite easily. Figure 5.15 shows the graphic without the tent in the background.

Figure 5.15: *What tent?*

The rotate tool

The **Rotate** tool is part of the **Modify** → **Transform** menu. This tool can be applied to the whole of a graphic or a selection of pixels. We will now describe how to **rotate** a graphic, but the explanation could just as easily be applied to a selection or layer.

If an image is rotated, it is spun around its centre point. Fireworks® gives you a few options for rotation. You can rotate by a fixed amount (180° or 90°) or you can decide by how much you rotate by choosing **Rotate** from the **Numeric Transform** menu. Remember that if an image is turned through a complete circle, so that it ends up facing exactly the same way as it did before (which would be a total waste of time), this is a 360° rotation. If the graphic ends up on its head, facing in the opposite direction, this is a 180° rotation.

The flip tool

Some students become confused between **rotating** and **flipping**. These are very different. The **Flip** tool will reverse a graphic so that the left-hand side of the original becomes the right-hand side of the new.

Figure 5.16: *From left to right: the original graphic; the original rotated by 90°; the original rotated by 270°; the original flipped horizontally.*

Adjusting image size

We have already discussed zooming into a graphic so that you can be more accurate. You may have used this tool when removing the tent from the background of the fire graphic. We explained that as you zoom in on a graphic you are changing not the size of the graphic, but how close you are to it. However, there will be times when you need to resize a graphic. This is likely to be when you import a graphic from another source, especially a digital camera.

Luckily, resizing is very straightforward. It is part of the **Modify** → **Canvas** menu.

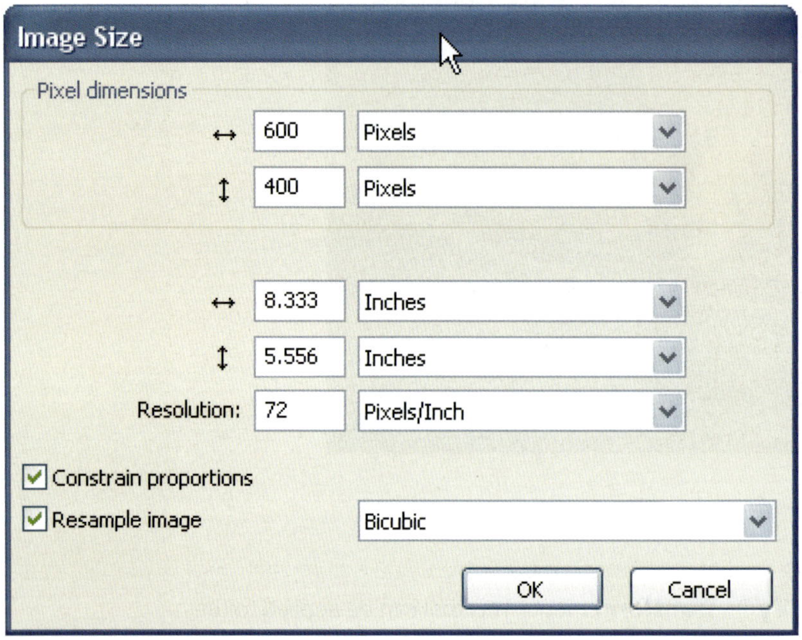

Figure 5.17: *The Modify Image Size menu.*

The settings are very much the same as the ones you use to create a graphic and so should be easy to use. The only concern you have is whether you want the proportions of your graphic to stay the same once you have resized it. If you do, make sure there is a tick in the **Constrain proportions** box. If you wish to change the relative proportions, remove this tick.

The *Return To Laughter* tour...

So far in this chapter, you have:

- cropped **Les and Des 1.jpg** to remove the parts of the original graphic that Les and Des did not want you to use
- created the Heads JPEG graphic.

Les and Des would like you to make some more changes.

Activity 11: Some final changes...

In this activity you will add some speech bubbles to the tour poster you have been working on.

- Create two graphics that have speech bubbles saying their famous catchphrase '**A funny thing happened to me in 1973**'.
- Add a speech bubble saying '**A funny thing happened to me**' to **Les and Des 9.jpg**.
- Add a speech bubble saying '**In 1973**' to **Les and Des 19.jpg**.

They would also like a map of the North of England, showing Blackpool, Preston, Barrow-in-Furness and Lancaster. They would like the map to use icons of the most famous tourist attraction in each of these locations to represent each town. They would like you to use the Blackpool Tower for Blackpool, but are happy for you to choose other icons for the three other locations.

- Research Preston, Barrow-in-Furness and Lancaster to find the most famous tourist attraction in each location.
- Use a range of geometric and freehand shapes to create the icon for Lancaster.
- Use any tool or technique to create the remaining icons.
- Create a new Fireworks® graphic that is 10 cm square. The background should be #66CCCC.
- Use the **Brush tool** to create the basic map.
- Add the icons (suitably scaled) to the graphic.
- Save your graphic in a suitable format.

And finally...

Always remember to check your work thoroughly before declaring it finally complete. You'll be surprised how many things you can tidy up to improve the quality! Chapter 6 explains how you should present your completed graphic.

CHAPTER 6

Assessment Objective 6

Present Work to a Client for a Specific Purpose, Using a Suitable Format for Display

Overview:

In this final chapter of this unit, we will discuss how best to present your work, as well as the other evidence you need to provide.

How this assessment objective will be assessed...

You will be assessed on the following aspects of your work:

- The choice of a suitable format to present your work.
- Evidence of having considered size, resolution, file type and colour mode in your choice of how to present your work.
- How well you justify your choice of medium to present your work.

Skills to use...

- You will need to present your work in a suitable format. While you could simply print out your work, this should be seen as the least impressive option.

How to achieve...

Pass requirements

P1 You will present your work in a suitable format.

P2 When creating your presentation, you will show some consideration of file size.

Merit requirements

M1 You will present your work in a suitable format.

M2 When creating your presentation, you will show consideration of file size, resolution and file type.

Distinction requirements

D1 You will present your work in a suitable format.

D2 When creating your presentation, you will show consideration of file size, resolution, file type and colour mode.

D3 You will justify your choice of medium to present the graphics.

Presenting your work

You should remember that if you were to be paid for the work you have done, your client would expect to see an impressive array of elements and it should look professional. If you present your work in a poor fashion, your client is less likely to be impressed, which would probably affect your chance of getting work in the future.

Unfortunately, you are not being paid for this work. However, this does not mean that your work does not need to be well presented. Below are a few design tips you may wish to use.

You can choose any suitable format in which to present your work, but those listed within the specifications are:

- a portfolio
- a slide presentation
- a report folder
- other.

The choice of format in which to present your work will, to some extent, depend on how skilled you are in working with other software applications. The report folder would seem the least impressive, as it is simply a printout of every graphic you create. However, it is the manner in which many graphic artists continue to present their work, and, as you are only graded for using a suitable format, you could simply print out the work and present it in a nice folder.

However, some imagination could be brought to bear. Your graphics are the result of many hours of hard work. How about presenting them as part of a digital portfolio, or as elements on a website? This will take a little more time, but, if you have the skills, these could be extremely impressive.

Finally, do not forget that if you are aiming for a **Distinction** grade, you must include in your work a justification for the presentation method used. There are many reasons you could use to explain your choice of medium. These may include that the client specifically asked for the work to be presented in a set format. However, it is far more likely that you will be given the choice of how to present your work. You could explain that, as your work is intended for inclusion on a poster or other printout, you have presented the work on paper. This would seem to be a perfectly reasonable explanation. However, you could explain that you want to set an upmarket image for your business and so all work is always presented digitally to the client. This explanation could also be used to justify a choice of high-quality paper as the print medium.

Activity 1: Create your portfolio of completed graphics...

In this activity you will present your completed elements.

- Using the format which best suits the grade for which you are aiming, present the work you have created for Les and Des.
- Provide evidence that you have considered size, resolution, file type and colour mode in your choice of presentation method.
- Justify your choice of presentation method.

Other considerations

The choice of how to present your work is only part of this final task. You must also show that you have taken account of the following factors.

- The size of the graphic (both physical size and file size). This could cover a range of issues, including how to present a physically very large graphic if you have one. If you are creating a graphic to be used as an A3 poster, should this graphic be presented as a small graphic or as large as the final graphic will appear on the poster? This is for you to decide and there is no right or wrong answer. However, you must show that this and similar issues have been considered.
- File types. You need to be aware of file types in your choice of presentation. It is possible, for example, that you may be asked to produce animated gifs. These are best presented in a format where the animation can be appreciated. If you chose to present these as a printed product, it is likely that your format would not be considered appropriate.
- Resolution. You may be asked to produce high-quality, high-resolution graphics. High-resolution graphics are best presented as a printout from a high-quality printer, rather than as an element on a screen.
- Colour mode. This is a relatively simple decision to make and is based around the simple point that things that look correct on a computer monitor do not always look so good on paper. This is especially true if you have used radiant colours. As part of your consideration of which format to use to present your work, a comparison of a printout of a graphic with the on-screen graphic would be a useful exercise.

Your evidence could take the form of a written report or maybe a diary. However you present it, you should aim to include all the considerations.

UNIT 5

Desktop Publishing

In this unit you will cover the following...

- AO1 **Plan a document to meet a given design brief for a document of at least *eight* A4 pages or equivalent**
- AO2 **Create styles**
- AO3 **Select and use tools in desktop publishing**
- AO4 **Use drawing tools included with DTP software to create basic shapes for inclusion in your completed publication**
- AO5 **Prepare publication for print**

CHAPTER 7

Assessment Objective 1

Plan a Document to Meet a Given Design Brief

Overview:

For this unit you will need to plan, draft, develop and then produce a high-quality document of eight A4 pages or equivalent. If you decide to produce a document with smaller pages the overall document will need to contain more pages. For example, an A5 document will need to contain 16 pages in order to require a similar amount of work and contain a similar amount of information.

It is assumed that you already have some familiarity with the use of Microsoft Publisher, the DTP package that will be used throughout the unit.

In this chapter you will study a range of existing documents and see how this information can be used to help design and plan your own document. For your portfolio you will come up with two alternative designs for your final document and choose the most appropriate one to develop to satisfy later Assessment Objectives. You will also look at alternative software that can be used to create documents and learn about planning to complete the project in the time available.

In order to complete the activities in this chapter you will need access to a number of additional files. These files are contained in the Unit 5 Student Resources zip file which can be downloaded from the OCR nationals in ICT (Units 3 & 5) Student Resources page on the Payne-Gallway website: www.payne-gallway.co.uk

How this assessment objective will be assessed...

You will be assessed on the following aspects of your work:

- Evidence of research, including a list of sources used for higher grades.
- Two alternative sets of sketch designs showing house style and overall page layout. Each set will take no more than two A4 pages.
- An explanation showing:
  - how your research influenced your designs
  - which design you have decided to complete
  - which software application you are going to use
  - a time plan for your project.

Skills to use...

You will not need to use any specific ICT skills to pass this Assessment Objective. Instead, this is where you will demonstrate:

- observation and analysis skills – identifying key points in professional documents that will help you design your own document
- design skills – planning alternative house styles and overall page layouts for your document
- organisational skills – writing up your design work, and planning your time.

How to achieve...

Pass requirements

P1 You will carry out limited research on a narrow range of organisations and end-users.

P2 You will provide limited evidence linking this research to your designs.

P3 You will produce basic plans which include:

- a few sketches
- identification of software to be used
- choice of final design
- some indication that time has been considered.

Merit requirements

M1 You will carry out independent research from a range of sources which you identify.

M2 You will provide evidence linking your research to the designs.

M3 You will produce plans to meet the requirements of the brief which include:

- sketches
- identification of software to be used
- choice of final design
- the timescale.

Distinction requirements

D1 You will carry out independent research from a wide range of sources which you identify.

D2 You will provide clear evidence linking your research to the designs.

D3 You will produce comprehensive design plans to meet fully the requirements of the brief which include:

- sketches
- identification of software to be used
- choice of final design
- a realistic timescale.

What is desktop publishing?

Essentially, desktop publishing (DTP) is the creation of documents by arranging text and graphics on pages. Although this can be done using word-processing software, specialist DTP packages offer a wider range of features to help you organise the layout of the pages. For example:

- Master pages, which allow you to set features that will appear on every page, or a selection of pages.
- Frames to contain text and graphics, so that they can be moved easily around the page. Text can flow from one frame to another.

- Layout guides, to help you position items more accurately.
- Layers, to allow you to place items on top of each other.

Commercial publishers use professional DTP packages, which have many more features than those available on the less expensive packages such as Microsoft Publisher and Serif PagePlus. However, these packages do have sufficient features to meet the requirements for this unit. These chapters have been written for Microsoft Publisher 2003. They can be used with other versions although some screenshots and methods may not exactly match those shown.

You will need to choose the software that you will use. It will not be appropriate to use word-processing software, as this will not allow you to use the more advanced DTP features that are needed. You may only have access to one DTP package, in which case that will be the one that you will use. There is no need for you to give any reasons for your choice.

The practice assignment

Throughout the unit, the following practice assignment will help you learn the skills you need.

Refer to the Unit 3 scenario on page 19. In the practice exercises for this unit you will be creating an eight-page souvenir programme for the 'Les and Des' comeback tour, which will be taking place next year. Some text and graphics will be provided for you, although you might also use graphics you created in Unit 3. You will also use some text from the Internet.

The programme needs to be A4 size with an attractive front cover. It needs to contain some information about Les and Des as individuals, details of their careers as a comedy act and of past tours, and details of venues and dates for the current tour, which is to be called 'Return to Laughter'. The programme needs to have plenty of photographs of Les and Des and lots of quotes from fans. Some adverts also need to be included.

Professional documents

Before you design your own document you need to examine some professional documents to identify some of the design features that are commonly used. You should look to see the range of fonts used, the way graphics and colour are used, and any other noticeable features.

For example, take a look at this book. You should notice the following:

- Text is in a single column, with a large right-hand margin.
- Colours are used to help particular features stand out – for example, activities are always on a purple background, key terms are always on a blue background. Yellow, red and green colour coding is used to identify Pass, Merit and Distinction requirements, respectively.
- Sans serif fonts are used throughout. Headings and sub-headings are in a slightly different font face and are larger.
- Bold text is used quite a lot to emphasise words. There is no use of underlining. Italic text is used for figure captions.
- Although the main text is on a white background, specific items, e.g. activities, are on coloured backgrounds. This makes them easy to find, and easily distinguishable from the rest of the text.
- Headers and footers are used to show the page number, unit number and chapter name in consistent places on a page.

Some of these features can be found on most professional documents. Others are peculiar to the particular design chosen for the book. The design chosen will always depend to some extent on the purpose of the document and the audience. An advertising brochure will have a very different design from a fiction book. A magazine aimed at children will be very different in appearance from one aimed at adults. However, there are some standard features that you will find on most documents:

- It is rare to find more than about three different font faces in the same document. Very often you will find just one for main text and one for headings.
- Most documents will use a fairly plain font face, although it is not unusual to see a fairly fancy (but readable) font for main headings.
- Underlining is almost never used to emphasise text in an electronic document, where it is often used to show hyperlinks.
- Most documents will adhere to a house style, including a limited range of colours and fonts. There may be a consistent feature such as a line, border, logo and/or simple graphic on each page.
- It is likely that there will be the same number of columns on each page, although there may be exceptions.

Key terms

Font face

A style of text, e.g. Times New Roman, Arial, etc. Also called the **typeface**.

Font

A font face, with size and styles (e.g. bold, italic) set.

Serif font

A type of font that has small 'feet' (called serifs) on the ends of each line, e.g. Times New Roman. This type of font is often used for small text, as it makes it easier to read.

Sans serif font

A type of font that does not have serifs, e.g. Arial. This is usually used for large text, although it is often used for small text too, as in this book.

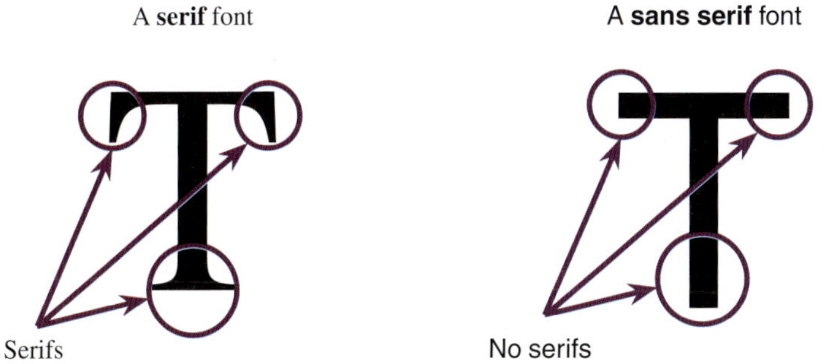

Figure 7.1: *Serif and sans serif fonts.*

Activity 1: Researching documents...

In this activity you will:

- look at the design features of a range of documents
- create evidence of research for your final portfolio.

- Collect some documents that you can use to help you learn about different design styles. You might be able to find, for example, newsletters, advertising leaflets, catalogues, brochures or programmes. You should try to collect at least four **different** types of document, from different organisations and aimed at different audiences.
- Open the file **Research form.doc**. This is a template for you to use to record your observations about the design features of the documents you have collected. It is located in the Forms folder. You will notice that the first row has been completed for you with comments about this book.
- Complete one row with comments about each document you have found. Add some more rows if necessary.
- Save and print your file.
- Open the file **Tour programmes.doc**.
- Look for some tour programmes on the Internet (try typing **"tour programmes"** into a search engine. Typing **"tour programmes" comedy** should help you find some programmes from comedy artists). You should try to look at two different programmes from at least two different bands/artists.
- Use the **tour programmes** template to note any features, on the covers or on the inside pages of the tour programmes, that you think are especially effective.
- Save and print your file.

Designing your publication

In this section you will consider design features to be used in your programme. You do not need to draw a design for each page, but you should make some decisions about, for example:

- colours
- font face, size, emphasis, alignment and leading
- columns
- graphics, including borders, lines, etc.
- paragraph spacing
- indents and tabs
- bullets

You will need to create sketches for the front cover and one inside page. You should not use more than two A4 pages for this.

You should be able to use some ideas that you have found from your research.

Figures 7.2 and 7.3 show two sketches for one possible design.

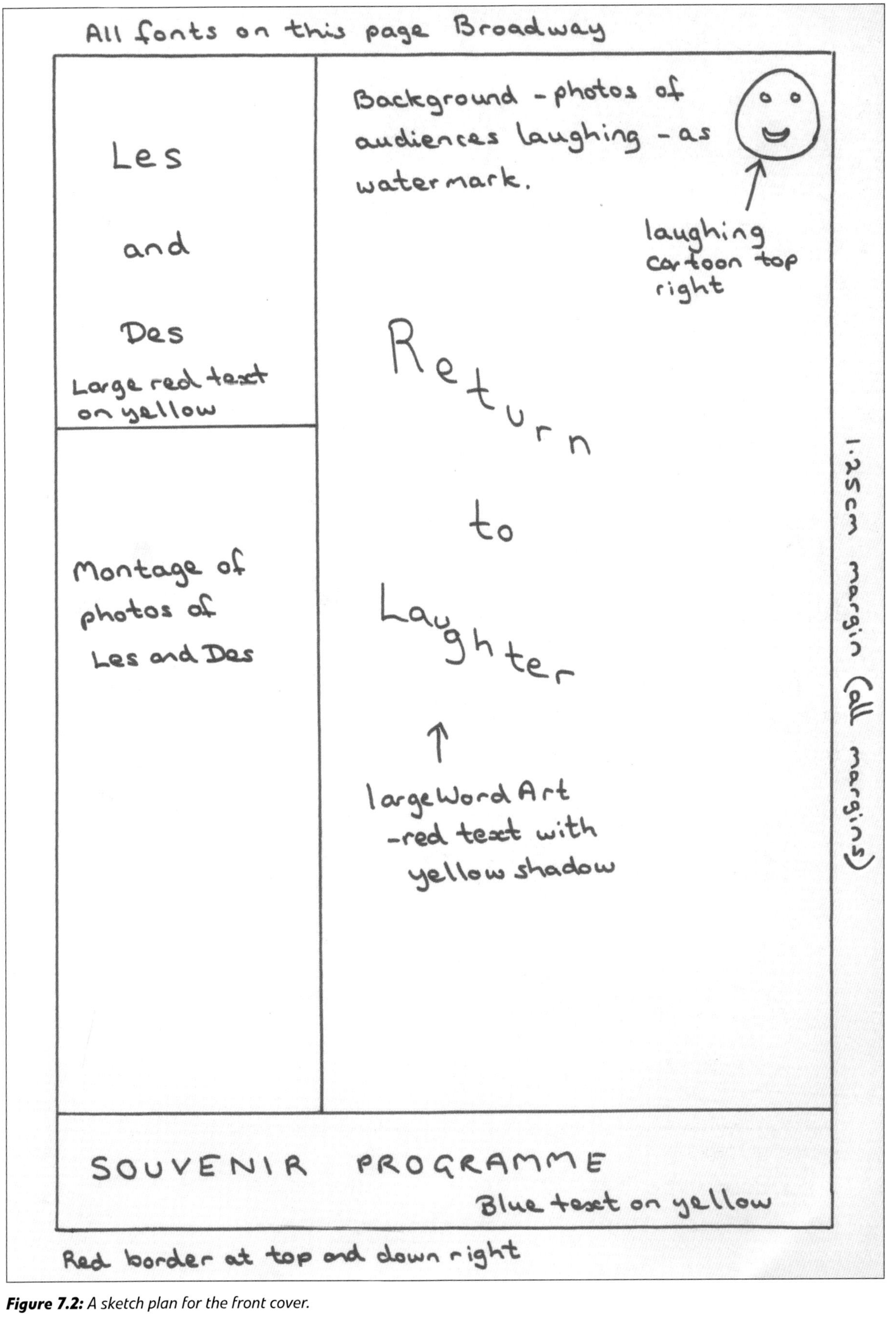

Figure 7.2: *A sketch plan for the front cover.*

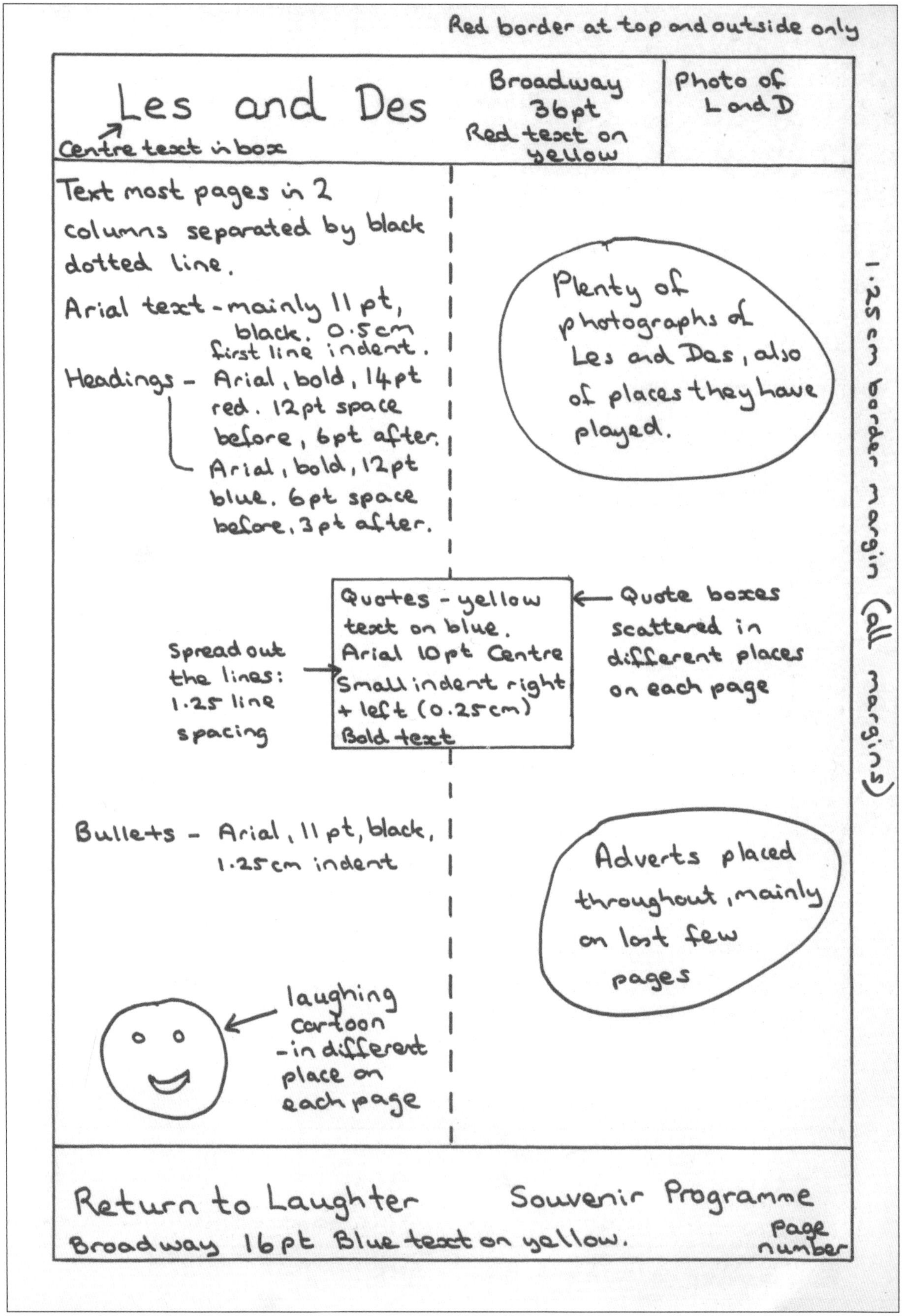

Figure 7.3: *A sketch plan for the basic layout of the other pages.*

Activity 2: Designing the pages...

In this activity you will create your own basic design for your publication.

- Refer back to the notes you made in Activity 1. Consider the features you thought were most effective.
- Make decisions and write down some rough notes about:
  - colours
  - fonts
  - borders
  - columns.
- Use pencil and paper to make a simple sketch of a design for a front cover for the programme for Les and Des.
- Now create a sketch design of the major design features for the other pages. You might not use this for **every** page, but it will show the main features that will be present on at least **most** of the other pages.
- Make sure that you have made clear on your design the colours, fonts, borders, columns, etc. that will be used.
- Compare your design with the one given in this chapter.
- Compare your design with those of other students, if possible.

Creating a time plan

Part of your preparation and design work must include a consideration of time. You will be given a set amount of time in which to complete your work for this unit. If you fail to produce an eight-page document in this time then you will not be able to pass the unit.

For a **Pass**, your plan might be quite simple, but for higher levels it will need to be more detailed, and for a **Distinction** it will need to be realistic.

One simple way of creating a time plan is to use a table, with dates for each week in the left-hand column, and what you will do each week in the right. This allows you to see how you need to split up your time and fit in all you need to do. A suitable template is provided for you in the Forms folder as **Time plan.doc**.

When you have completed the practice assignment in these chapters you will be able to create a realistic time plan for your assessed publication.

Portfolio builder

For your portfolio you will need to create **two** alternative designs, such as those given in this chapter and created in Activity 2.

You should include in your portfolio:

- Evidence of the research you have carried out. You may include here the work you produced for Activity 1, to which you can add research from other publications if necessary. You should definitely include evidence of some research into the type of publication you are going to produce yourself.

- Four sides of A4 with sketches showing your two alternative designs. For each design you should show the front page and a sample inside page.
- An explanation (this could be a written/word processed document) which shows:
  - how your research influenced your design choices (for a **Pass** you might just explain this to your teacher)
  - which design you have chosen to use in your publication
  - the name of the particular piece of software you will be using; you do not have to give any reason why
- Your time plan, showing how you will complete your eight-page document in the time you have available.

You will access the higher grades by:

- choosing for yourself a wide range of documents for your research – different types of document aimed at different types of audience
- clearly showing that your research has influenced your designs
- including all relevant details in your designs, e.g. colours, fonts, columns, graphics – your front page should be detailed and your other page should clearly show the main features that will be consistent on most other pages
- creating a realistic time plan that considers all the tasks you will need to do
- making sure that your plans meet the requirements of the given brief.

CHAPTER 8

Assessment Objective 2

Create Styles

Overview:

In this chapter you will learn about the use of **styles** to allow you easily to format different types of text, e.g. main headings, sub-headings and body text. You will define some text styles for use in your publication.

You will be following the programme designs in Figures 7.2 and 7.3 from Chapter 7.

How this assessment objective will be assessed...

You will be assessed on the following aspects of your work:

- Screenshots showing the styles defined.
- The range of aspects defined for each style will affect whether or not a **Pass**, **Merit** or **Distinction** will be awarded.
- The appropriateness of the styles will also affect the grade awarded.

Skills to use...

You will learn to set the following aspects in the styles you create:

- Font (face, size, emphasis, alignment and leading)
- Paragraph spacing
- Indents and tabs
- Bullets

How to achieve...

Pass requirements

P1 You will create three different styles.

P2 Each style will include at least one aspect from each of the following:

- Font (face, size, emphasis, alignment or leading)
- Paragraph spacing
- Indents or tabs.

Merit requirements

M1 You will create three different styles.

M2 Each style will include the full range of aspects from each of the following:

- Font (face, size, emphasis, alignment and leading)
- Paragraph spacing
- Indents or tabs.

M3 The styles will mostly be fit for purpose.

Distinction requirements

D1 You will create three different styles.

D2 Each style will include the full range of aspects from each of the following:

- Font (face, size, emphasis, alignment and leading)
- Paragraph spacing
- Indents or tabs
- Bullets.

D3 The styles will be fit for purpose.

What are styles?

You should already have noticed that in any professional publication there will be a consistent format for different types of text, for example:

- **main headings** – these need to stand out well at the beginning of a new section/chapter
- **sub-headings** – there may be a number of different levels of sub-heading, each standing out from the main text: each level will be a defined size
- **body text** – this is the main text of the document
- **labels** for graphics.

It is possible to simply format each heading and label separately, but this might take a number of actions, defining the font face, size, style, colour, alignment, etc. A much more efficient method is to define **styles** before you create your document, then simply select the style you need each time.

Even if you don't set any styles yourself there will be one style already set – **Normal**. This is the default style, the one that you will get if you don't change any formatting. When you first load Microsoft Publisher the Normal style will be Times New Roman, 10 point, regular font style (not bold or italic), not underlined, black, left aligned, single line spacing with no bullets, numbering, indents or tabs set. You can change this to match whatever you want the main style to be.

Setting and changing styles

In Microsoft Publisher, to set new styles or to change existing ones, click **Format** from the toolbar and click **Styles and Formatting…**.

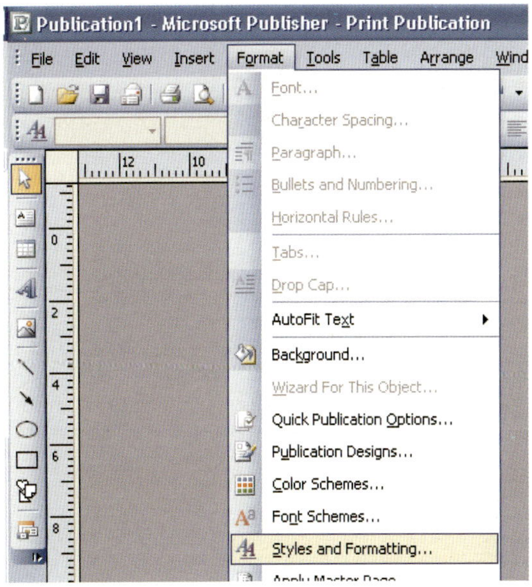

Figure 8.1: *Choosing styles and formatting.*

To create a new style, click the **Create new style** button at the bottom of the **Styles and Formatting** window that appears on the left.

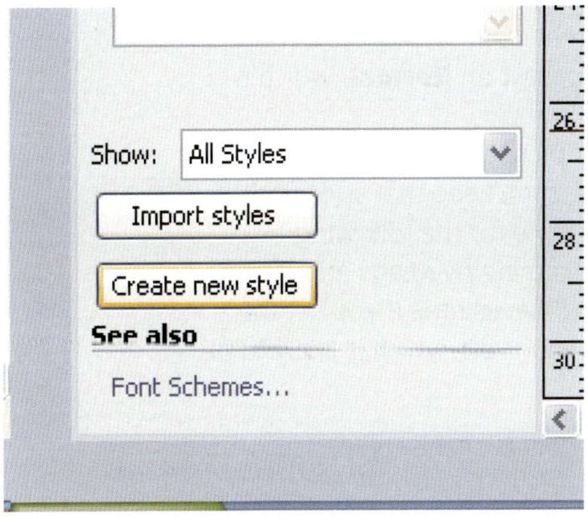

Figure 8.2: *Creating a new style.*

You will then be shown a dialogue box from where you can define all the settings for your new style (see Figure 8.3).

Figure 8.3: *Defining a style.*

On the left you need to make three choices:

- Enter a name for the style – this will usually be one or two words, which you will use to recognise the style. For example **Body text**, **Main heading**, **Large sub-heading**, **Small sub-heading**, **Graphic labels, bulleted list**, etc.
- Choose a style to base your new one on. While it does not really matter what this is, it will save you time if you choose the one which most closely matches the settings you want. When you are defining your first style then you will have to base it on **Normal**, which is the only one available.
- Choose a style for the following paragraph. Styles affect complete paragraphs, not individual words or characters. Often you want to set a style, then keep that style until you choose something different. If so, you choose the same style for the following paragraph, which is the default. However, some styles, for example headings and labels, are almost always only needed for one line or paragraph, so it saves time if you set the following paragraph to the style you use for the majority of your text, which is likely to be **Body text**.

On the right are buttons that allow you to change the various aspects of the style:

- **Font**. Here you can choose the font face, style (this is referred to in the unit as the 'emphasis' – regular, bold and/or italic), size, underline style and colour. You can also choose to make your font superscript, subscript, outline, embossed, small caps, all caps, shadow or engrave.
- **Character spacing**. This is not often changed, and is not required in this unit. It allows you to horizontally shrink or stretch characters and to change the space between the characters.
- **Paragraph**. This allows you to adjust the alignment (left, right, centred), paragraph indents, spacing before and after the paragraphs and spacing between the lines (called **leading**).

- **Bullets and numbering**. This allows you to define the layout (e.g. how far the list item is indented) and style (bullet graphic, number, etc.) of lists.
- **Horizontal rules**. Here you can set ruled lines before and/or after a paragraph. Although not used in many styles, this can be effective to emphasise particular paragraphs or headings.
- **Tabs** allows you to set tab stops, choosing the position, type of tab (left, right, centre, decimal) and any leader (perhaps confusingly, this is pronounced 'leeder', as it refers to leading characters that fill in the space when you press the **tab** key).

Key term

Leading

Leading (pronounced 'ledding') is an old printing term, used because space between lines used to be created by adding strips of lead underneath lines of text.

You can set many aspects of a style. The best way to understand all of them is to experiment by creating some different styles, choosing a range of different aspects. You will soon get a feel for what they offer.

Activity 1: Setting styles in Microsoft Publisher...

In this activity you will:

- create a new Publisher document
- edit the normal style
- set a variety of different styles suitable for the Les and Des programme, following the design plans in Figures 7.2 and 7.3
- use the styles you have created.

➔ Open Microsoft Publisher and choose **Blank Publications** and **Full Page**.

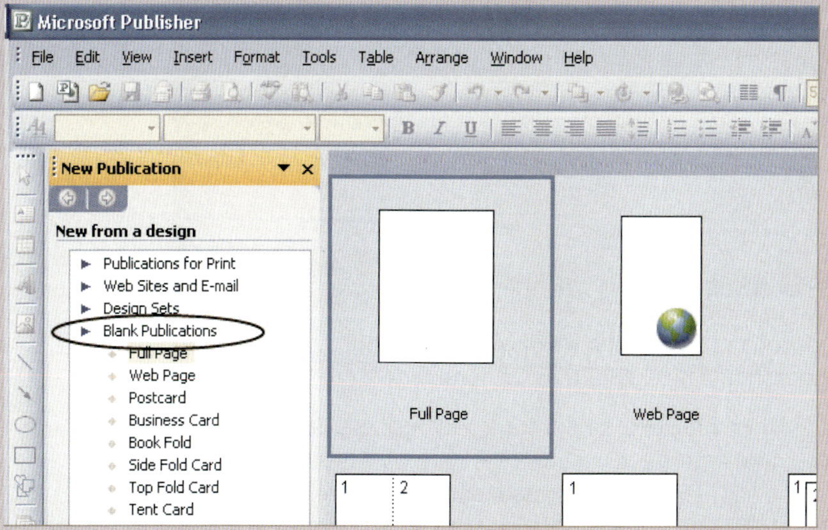

Figure 8.4: Starting a new Publisher document.

Publisher offers you a range of pre-designed templates, which you don't want, so close down the **Publication Designs** window that is displayed.

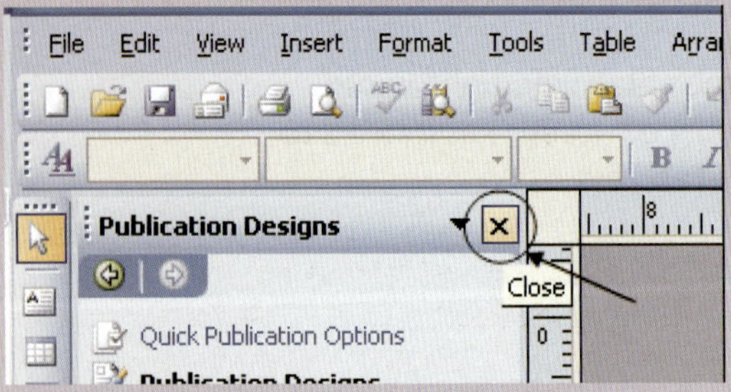

Figure 8.5: *Closing down the Publication Designs window.*

The plan in Figure 7.3 shows that the main text is to be Arial, size 11 point.

Choose **Format** from the toolbar and click **Styles and Formatting...**.

When you start a new document there will probably be only one style showing in the **Styles and Formatting** window on the left: **Normal**. This is the style for normal text, which we need to change to Arial, 11 point.

Click the drop-down menu arrow next to **Normal**, then choose **Modify...**.

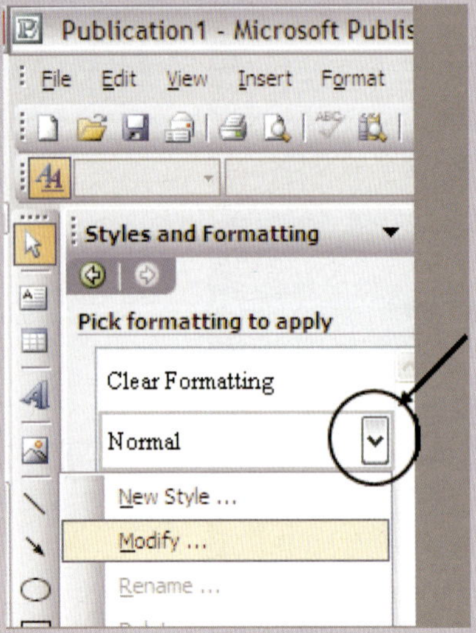

Figure 8.6: *Modifying the **Normal** style.*

Use the **Font...** button to select **Arial**, **11 point** size, then click **OK** twice.

While it is common to change the font and size for the **Normal** style, it is not a good idea to change any other features. These should be changed by creating other styles.

Although the paragraphs in this book are **blocked**, as is common in business documents, many newspapers, magazines and newsletters use indented paragraphs. This allows paragraphs to be closer together and still be clearly separated, so saving space. In the publication you design for your portfolio you can decide which style to use, but for the programme for Les and Des we will use indented paragraphs, with a 6 point (half-line) space between each.

Key term

Blocked

A paragraph is described as a blocked paragraph when the first line is not indented.

TIP

It is acceptable in a DTP document to *either* indent paragraphs slightly *or* to leave a paragraph space between paragraphs. You should *not* do both.

- Click the **Create new style** button and create a style called **Body text**. This will be used for the main text on each page. Choose to base this on **Normal** and choose **Body text** for the following paragraph.
- Use the **Paragraph...** button to choose a **First line** indent of **0.5cm** and a **6 point** space **after** the paragraph. Click **OK**. (It is good practice to apply widow and orphan control to body text. We cover this in Chapter 9, pages 88–89.)

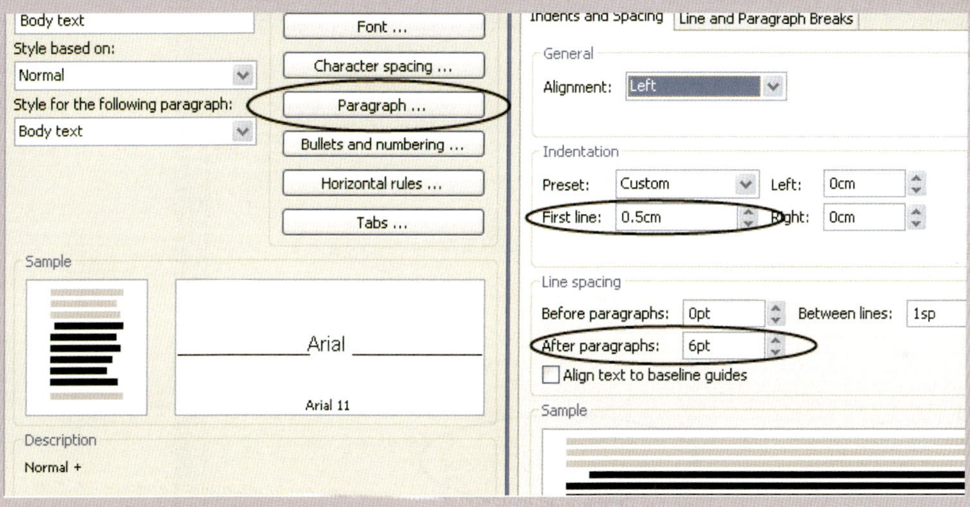

Figure 8.7: *Paragraph settings for body text.*

- Click the **Create new style** button and create a style called **LD Header**. This will be the style for the **Les and Des** at the top of each standard page. Choose to base this on **Normal** and choose **Body text** for the following paragraph.
- Use the **Font** button to choose **Broadway**, **36** point, **red**, then click **OK**.
- Use the **Paragraph...** button to choose **Center** alignment and **10** point space **before** and **after** the paragraph. Click **OK**.
- Now create a second style, called **LD Footer**, for the text at the bottom of each standard page. Base this on the **Normal** style and change the **Font** to **Broadway**, **16** point, **blue**.
- To get the text **Souvenir Programme** at the right-hand side you need a right tab. Set this at **17.8cm**, which is just less than the width of the frame shown on the plan:

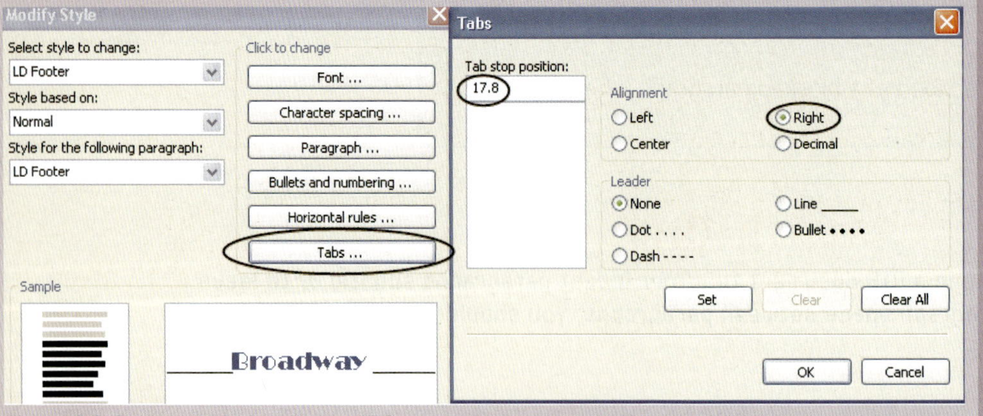

Figure 8.8: *Setting a right-hand tab at 17.8 cm.*

We will now create a new style for the main headings on the main pages.

- Create the new style and name it **Main Heading**. Base this on **Normal** style and set the style for the following paragraph to **Body text**.
- Set the **Font** to **Arial**, **bold**, **14** point, **red**.
- Use the **Paragraph** button to set the **space before** to **12** point and the **space after** to **6** point. This give a little more space above and below the headings, to help them stand out more and to separate different items.

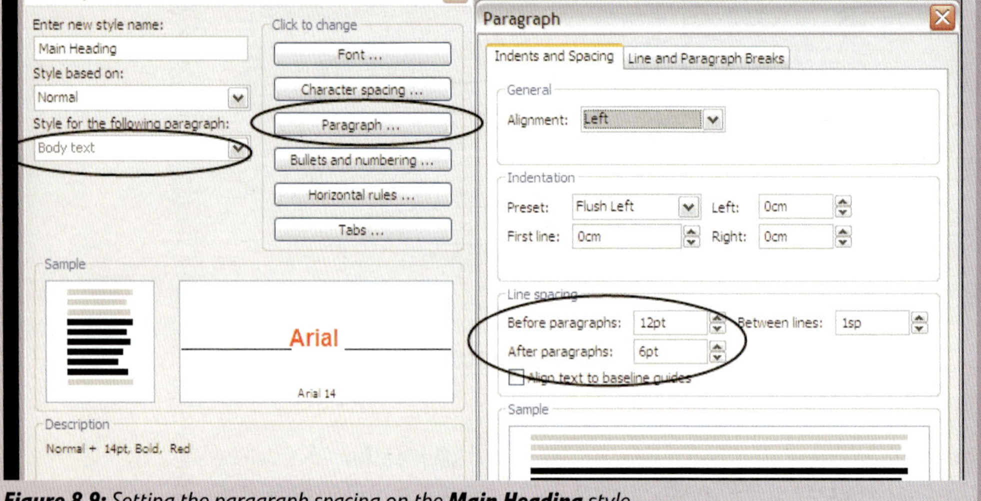

Figure 8.9: *Setting the paragraph spacing on the* ***Main Heading*** *style.*

We can now create a new style for the sub-headings on the main pages.

- Create the new style and name it **Sub Heading**. Base this on the **Main Heading** style, as this is quite similar. Set the style for the following paragraph to **Body text**.
- Change the font size to **12** point and the colour to **blue**.
- Change the **Space before paragraph** to **6** point and the **space after** to **3**. (To apply 'keep with next' to sub-headings see Chapter 9, pages 88–89.)

We now need a style for the quotes.

- Create the new style and name it **Quotes**. Base it on **Normal** style and set the style for the following paragraph to **Quotes**. This will allow quotes to have more than one paragraph.
- Set the **font** to **Arial**, **10** point, **bold**, **yellow**.
- Use the **Paragraph** button to set the space **Between lines** (the leading) to **1.25** spacing. Set **Left** and **Right** indentations to **0.25cm**.

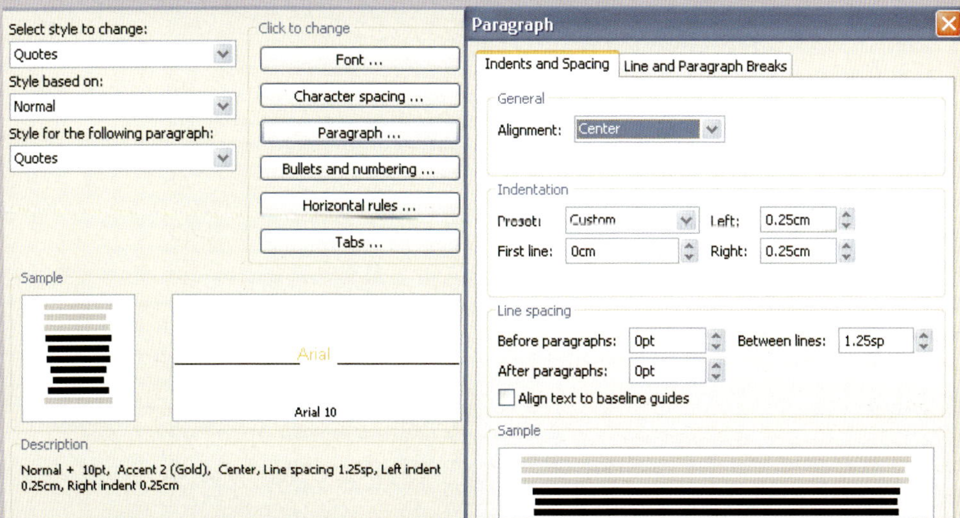

Figure 8.10: *Paragraph settings for the* ***Quotes*** *style.*

Now you have set the main styles that you need you can experiment using them.

- Use the **Text box** tool to drag out a text frame at the top of your blank document. The exact size and shape doesn't matter – it is just to practise using the styles.

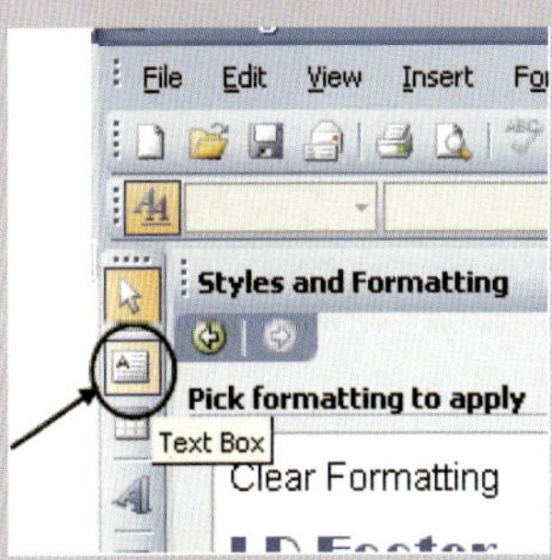

Figure 8.11: *The* ***Text box*** *tool*

- You will probably want to change the zoom to at least 100% so that you can see the text you enter.
- Type in some text. You should see that this is formatted in Arial, 11 point, as you defined the normal style to be. Press **Enter** when you have finished.
- Click the **LD Header** style in the style window and type in some text. You should see that the text is formatted according to the style you set.
- Press **Enter** and type some more text. You should see that this has automatically been set back to **Body text**.

- Now click one of the other styles, without pressing **Enter**. You should see that this automatically changes the paragraph you are typing to the style you have set.
- Experiment using and changing the different styles until you are confident in their use.
- When you have finished experimenting, right click inside the text box and choose **Delete Object** to delete the text box.

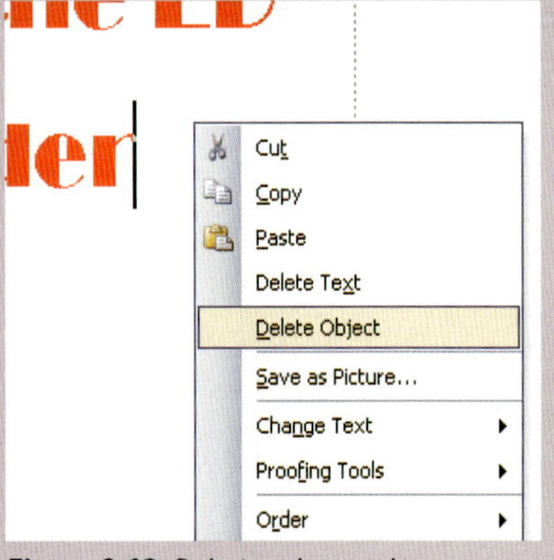

Figure 8.12: *Deleting the text box.*

- Save the file, so that you save the styles you have set, even though you have not created anything visible on the pages.

Portfolio builder

For your portfolio you will need to provide evidence that you have set at least three styles for your publication. These should match the plans you created for Assessment Objective 1.

For each style you should set:

- the font – choose the face, size and emphasis (bold, italic, underlined, etc.)
- paragraph settings – choose the alignment (left, centre, right), leading (space between lines), indents and paragraph spacing (space between paragraphs)
- tabs
- bullets (for **Distinction** grade).

Realistically you will not need to alter all of these settings for all of your styles. For example, many styles will need to be left aligned, not bold or italic, with normal paragraph spacing. However, you should show that you have *considered* all of these options and deliberately chosen to leave some unchanged. In order to **Pass** this objective you must ensure that you change the font, paragraph spacing and indents or tabs at least once.

Refer to the '**How to achieve**' section at the beginning of this chapter, which outlines the requirements for each grade for this objective. It is up to you to demonstrate your ability to change the required range of settings. If that means creating more than three styles then that is what you should do.

Although the styles you set will be accessible from your final file you should also provide annotated screenshot evidence for each style you create. This will allow you to show that you have considered each of the required aspects for each style. It will also allow you to explain why each aspect is appropriate for each particular style for your publication. This will help you gain the higher grades. There is a template called **Styles.doc** available in the Forms folder for you to use to help you lay out this work if you wish. Create a new document for each style, then add a screenshot to column 2 and an explanation to column 3 for each aspect. An example of the first page of a completed sheet is shown in Figure 8.13.

Styles

Style Name:	Quotes	
Font	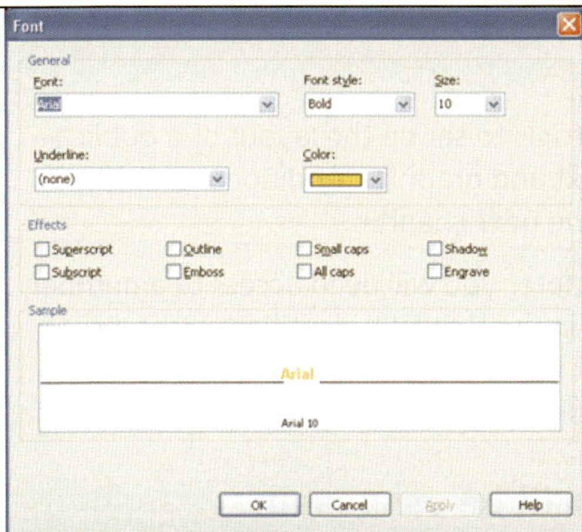	I chose yellow and bold to stand out against the blue background I'll be having for the quotes. These will all be short pieces of text in small blue text boxes. They will be size 10, which is slightly smaller than the main text, because they are just little extras.
Paragraph	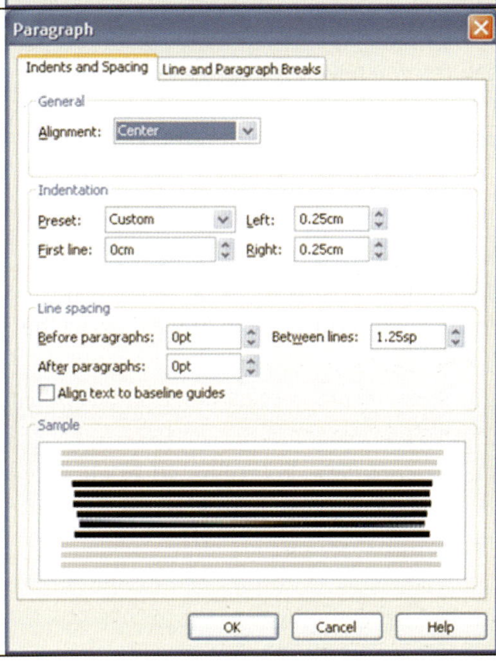	I chose left and right margins of 0.25cm so that the text would not go right to the edge of the blue background. I also chose Center, because this will make the short quotes look best against the blue background. I also chose 1.25 spacing so that the text wasn't too crammed together, making it easier to read.
Bullets and numbering		I didn't want any bullets or numbering as the quotes will often only be one or two lines.

Figure 8.13: *Annotating a style using the* ***Styles*** *template.*

Remember that you can always modify styles later, and that any modifications will affect all the text you have already used for that style. If you do modify your style during your work for any reason, there is no need to redo this section of your portfolio, just add a page explaining the modification you have made and why you made it.

CHAPTER 9

Assessment Objective 3

Select and Use Tools in Desktop Publishing

Overview:

In this chapter you will use a range of DTP tools to set up the layout of a publication. You will then enter text and import text and graphics. Additional graphics to complete the publication will be added in the next chapter.

In order to complete the activities in this chapter you will need access to a number of additional files. These files are contained in the Unit 5 Student Resources zip file which can be downloaded from the OCR nationals in ICT (Units 3 & 5) Student Resources page on the Payne-Gallway website: www.payne-gallway.co.uk

How this assessment objective will be assessed...

You will be assessed on the following aspects of your work:

- Your final publication will show some of the features you have used, and the overall quality and appropriateness of this publication will be assessed.
- Screenshots may be used to demonstrate some of the features used in setting up the publication.

Skills to use...

You will learn to define and use master pages in Microsoft Publisher to set general layout features such as margins, headers and footers. You will then add text and graphics to fill the eight pages of your publication. In doing this you will:

- set and use layout guides
- type in text
- create and edit WordArt text (we look at WordArt in more detail in Chapter 10 as it is a requirement for AO4)
- import text and graphics
- link text frames
- add a graphic as a watermark
- set hyphenation
- use the spelling and design checkers to check your publication.

How to achieve...

Pass requirements

P1 You will produce a simple eight-page publication using a DTP package.

P2 You will use some DTP facilities to lay out your publication.

P3 You will import text and graphics as well as entering some text of your own.

Merit requirements

M1 You will produce a detailed eight-page publication, using a DTP package, which mostly meets the demands of the brief.

M2 You will make good use of DTP facilities to lay out your publication.

M3 You will make good use of imported text and graphics as well as entering some text of your own.

Distinction requirements

D1 You will produce a detailed eight-page publication, using a DTP package, which fully meets the demands of the brief.

D2 You will make good use of DTP facilities to lay out your publication. All will be used appropriately.

D3 You will make good use of imported text and graphics as well as entering some text of your own. All will be used appropriately.

Setting up a DTP publication by creating master pages

In Chapter 8 we started to set up a DTP publication by setting appropriate styles for use in the Les and Des programme. The next stage is to set up the layout of the pages by defining:

- margins
- layout guides to help position items accurately
- headers and footers
- any other features that are to appear on a number of pages.

You may be familiar with the use of presentation or web-design software, where a template or theme can be selected or created, which defines the basic features of all new pages. In Publisher this function is carried out by defining **Master Pages**. This is more flexible than a simple template, as you can define a number of different master pages, for example one for each chapter of a book. You can also choose to ignore the master page(s) for a particular page, if you have a reason for wanting a different layout for that page.

To create a master page in Publisher you open up the file (or start a new one) and choose **View** → **Master Page**. A new pane called **Edit Master Pages** will open up and show you that there is one master page available: **Master Page A**, which is now showing. You can either alter this one or create a new one using the **New Master Page...** button at the bottom of the pane.

Anything you add to this page (e.g. guidelines, backgrounds, graphics, text, headers, footers, etc.) will appear on every page of your publication.

TIP

A quick way of moving between the master page and normal view is to press **Ctrl + M**.

Activity 1: Setting up the master page...

In this activity you will set up a master page with the following:

- Margins
- Layout guides
- A header and a footer
- Page numbers

➲ Load the Publisher file you created in Chapter 8.

➲ Although you will not be printing yet, it is important to set the correct printer driver before you start the document, as different driver settings can alter the layout of your page. To do this, select **File** from the menu bar, then choose **Page Setup...** and choose the correct printer you will be using from the **Printer and Paper** tab. Click on **OK**.

You are now ready to set up the master page for the publication you are going to create for Les and Des.

➲ Choose **View** from the menu bar and click **Master Page**.

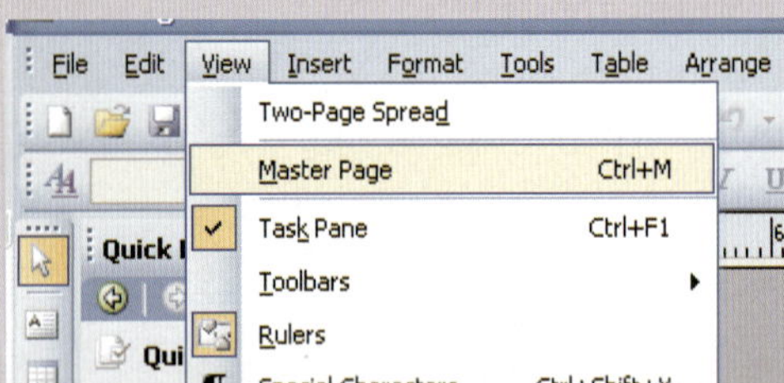

Figure 9.1: *Viewing a Master Page.*

The blank page you see is the blank master page, **Master A**, which you are now going to change.

➲ You should be able to see, by looking at the rulers along the top and left edges of the main working area, that the margins are currently set at just over 2 cm.

TIP

If you can't see these rulers, use the View menu to make sure that the Rulers option is turned on. If the rulers are showing the margins set at about 1 unit then your system is probably set to inches. You can change this by using Tools → Options... and changing the units on the General tab, as shown in Figure 9.2.

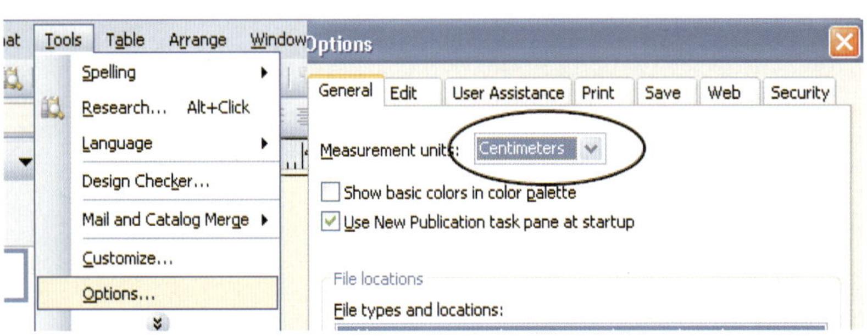

Figure 9.2: *Setting the measurement units to centimetres.*

Ordinary laser and inkjet printers cannot print right to the edge of the paper, so there must be a margin. However, it does not need to be 2 cm wide, 1–1.5 cm is much more usual, depending on the requirements of the printer.

- Our plans for the Les and Des programme show a margin of 1.25 cm. Set this by clicking **Arrange** on the toolbar, choosing **Layout Guides...** and altering the values for each margin.

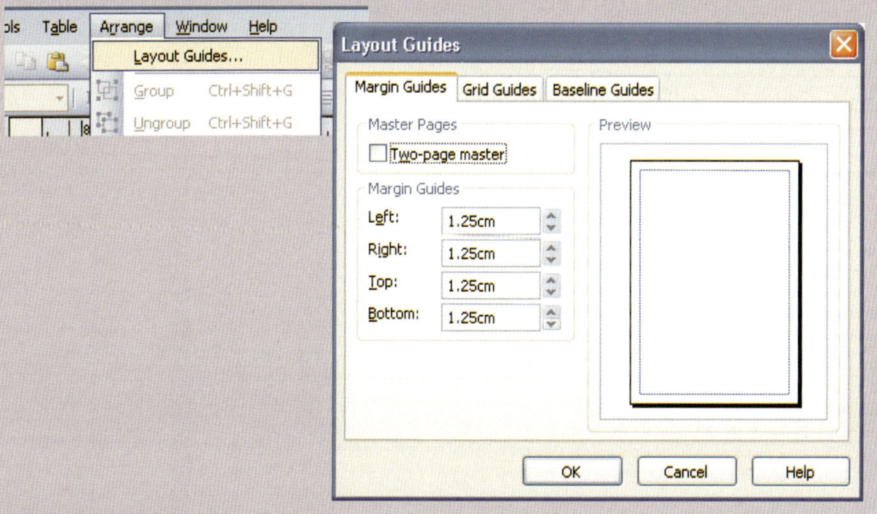

***Figure 9.3:** Changing the page margins.*

The plan for our programme shows text in two columns. To get these columns exactly the right size and in exactly the right place we will use some **layout guides**. These do not print, but will help you position items.

- In the **Layout Guides** dialogue box, select the **Grid Guides** tab. Choose **2** columns and set the spacing between them to **0.5**.

- Although we have no plans to split up the pages horizontally, it can be very useful to have some horizontal guides too. These can help, for example, if we want to position two graphics side by side. Choose **12** horizontal guides and set the spacing between these (called the **gutter**) to **0** as shown in Figure 9.4.

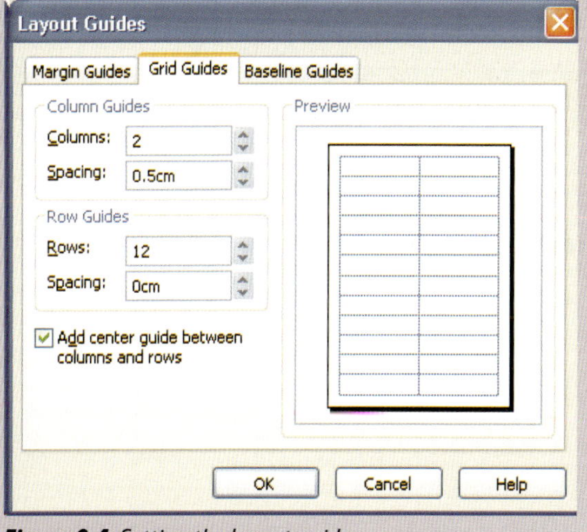

***Figure 9.4:** Setting the layout guides.*

TIP

When adding text and graphics in columns you should always leave a gutter between them. If columns are too close together they look cluttered and are difficult to read.

- Create a header by making a text frame at the top of the page. Allow this to click onto the first 'row' of the layout guides and take it across to about 15 cm.

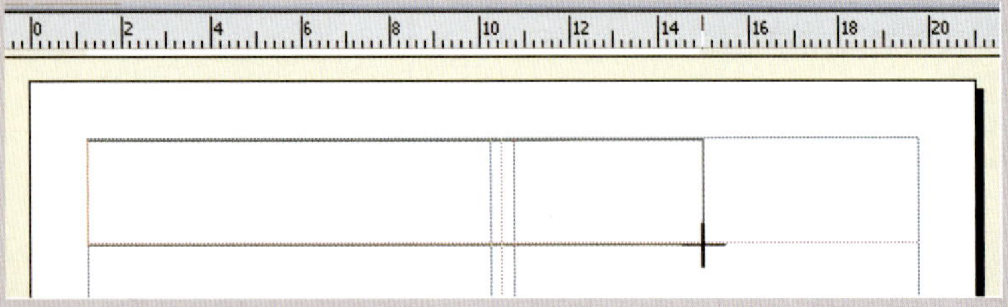

Figure 9.5: *Creating a text frame for the heading.*

- Choose **Format** from the menu bar, then **Styles and Formatting...** and select the **LD Header** style you created in Chapter 8.

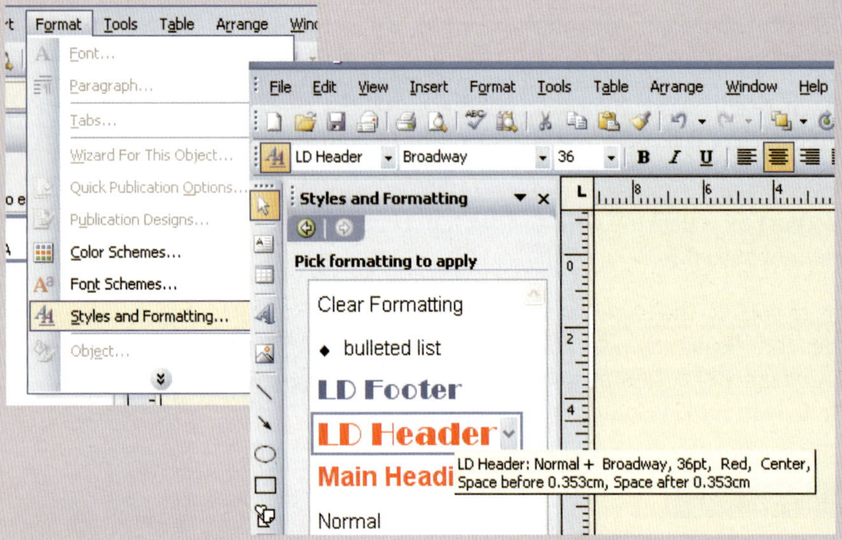

Figure 9.6: *Selecting the* ***LD Header*** *style.*

- Type in the text **Les and Des**.
- Use the **Fill Color** tool on the toolbar to change the fill colour to **yellow**. This can also be done by right clicking and choosing **Format Text Box...**.

You now need to insert a photograph at the right-hand side of this frame.

- Click the **Picture Frame** tool and choose **Picture from File**.

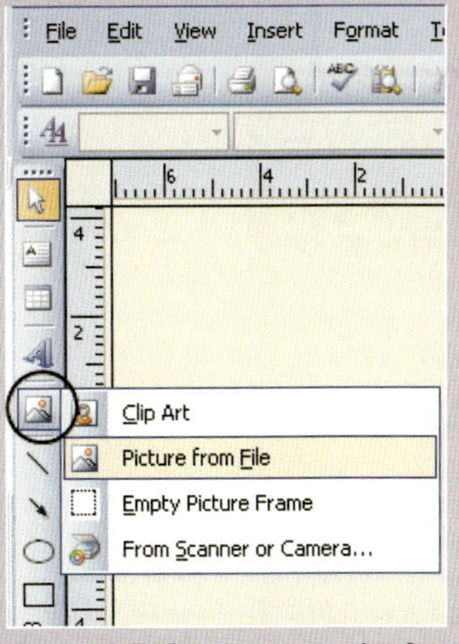

Figure 9.7: *Creating a graphic frame for a picture stored as a file.*

- Drag out a frame in the space to the right of the text frame you have just created. Don't worry that you can't get it to the right size and shape – this will be altered when you have imported the picture.
- Select the photograph **LesanddesHeader** from **OCR Level 2 Nationals Unit 5 Student Resources → Photos → Les and Des**.
- Resize the frame and move it so that it fits in the top right corner. Make sure you only use the **corner** handles to resize the photograph, so that you don't distort it.
- Increase the width of the text frame so that it touches the photograph. You may need to zoom in to allow you to set the frame sizes accurately. Your header should now resemble Figure 9.8.

TIP

Always resize photographs using the corner handles only. If you want to change the shape of the photograph, **crop** it rather than resizing.

Figure 9.8: *The completed heading.*

- You should now be able to create a footer matching the plan in Figure 7.3. Remember to use the **LD Footer** style, and press the **Tab** key after typing 'Return to Laughter', so that 'Souvenir Programme' is aligned to the right of the frame (see Figure 9.9).

Figure 9.9: *The bottom border.*

- Create a small text frame at the bottom right-hand corner of the footer. Choose the **LD Footer** style and then choose to centre the text by clicking the **Center** tool on the formatting toolbar.
- Click **Insert** on the menu bar and choose **Page Numbers...**. Keep the choice of **Current text box** and untick the box to show that you do **not** want to **Show page number on first page**.

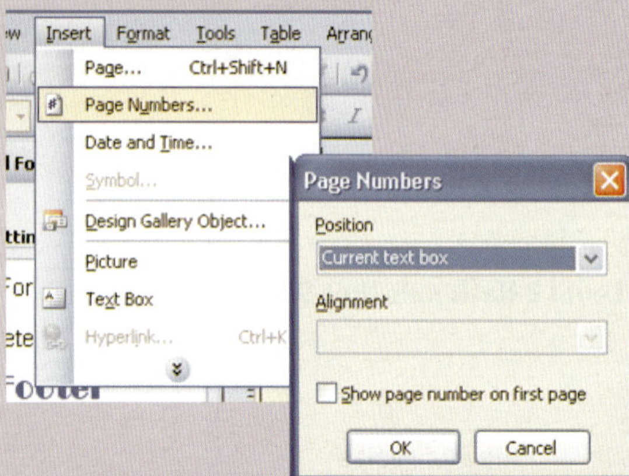

Figure 9.10: *Inserting a page number into a text frame.*

- Click the **Close Master View** button on the **Edit Master Pages** toolbar, then save your publication.

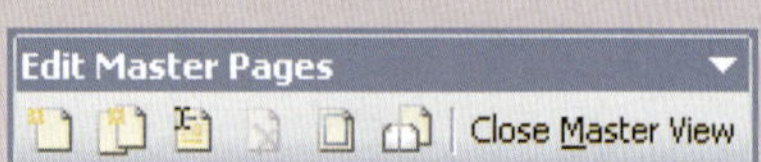

Figure 9.11: *Closing the Master View.*

Creating a two-page master page

Look at the layout of this book. You will see that there are headers and footers on each page, but that they are in different places on the two pages facing each other. This can easily be achieved in Publisher by using master pages – set the features as you want to see them on the right-hand page, using a different frame for each item, then change to a two-page master by clicking the **Change Single-Page/Two-Page** button on the **Edit Master Pages** toolbar.

Changing to a two-page master will create a left-hand page which mirrors the one you have created. If you want to make changes later it is often better to change back to a single page, make the alterations, then change back to a double page again. However, once you have a two-page master you can change items on either page to create further differences between the two pages.

Activity 2: Creating a two-page master...

In this activity you will:

- convert your master page into a two-page master
- change your footer so that the text is mirrored on the pages
- add extra pages to your publication.

➔ Load the publication you saved at the end of Activity 1 and show the **master page** by pressing **Ctrl + M** or using **View → Master Page**.

➔ Click the **Change Single-Page/Two-Page** button on the **Edit Master Pages** toolbar to transform your master page into a two-page master.

➔ Look carefully at the two pages that are now displayed. You may need to use the zoom tools on the toolbar to reduce the scale so that you can see them clearly.

You should see that the two pages are the same, except that the frames are positioned as mirror images, so that the photograph in the header is always on the outside edge. The page numbers are positioned likewise at the bottom of the page. The photograph has also been mirrored. However, you may be surprised to see that the text in the footer has not been reversed. This is because it was all entered into one frame.

You can reverse the footer by putting the two pieces of text into two different frames.

➔ Click the **Change Single-Page/Two-Page** button on the **Edit Master Pages** toolbar again, to convert your master page back to a single-page master. You will be asked to confirm that you really want to do this. Click **OK**.

➔ Delete the text **Souvenir Programme** from the footer.

➔ Drag in the right-hand edge of the text frame so that it is only just wide enough to contain the text, as shown in Figure 9.12.

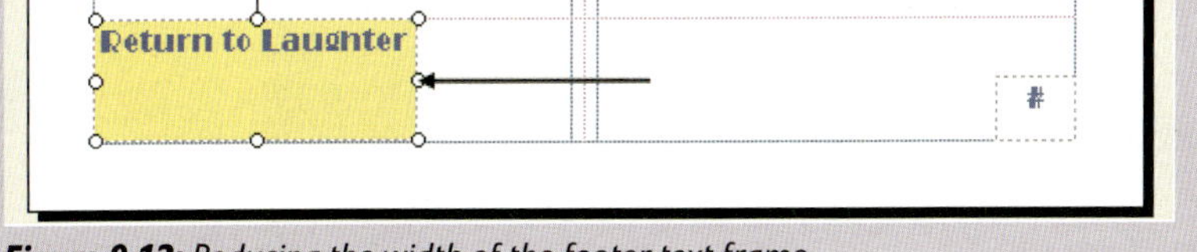

***Figure 9.12:** Reducing the width of the footer text frame.*

➔ Right click inside this text frame and choose **Copy**. Now right click again and choose **Paste** to give you a second copy of the text frame.

➔ Move the new text frame to the right-hand side of the page, by dragging one of its edges.

You may have noticed that the page number disappeared when you moved the text frame. It has not been deleted – it's just been covered up.

➔ Right click the right-hand text frame and choose **Order → Send to Back**.

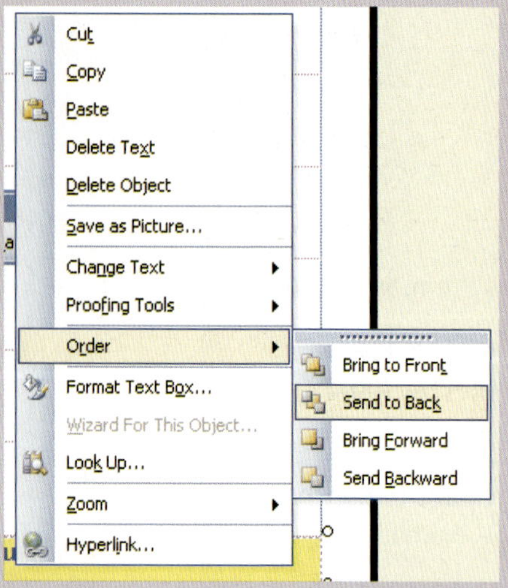

Figure 9.13: *Moving the text frame to the back, so that you can see the page number.*

- Replace the text in the right-hand box with **Souvenir Programme**. Increase the width of the box by dragging the left-hand edge out, until it is just wide enough to contain the text.

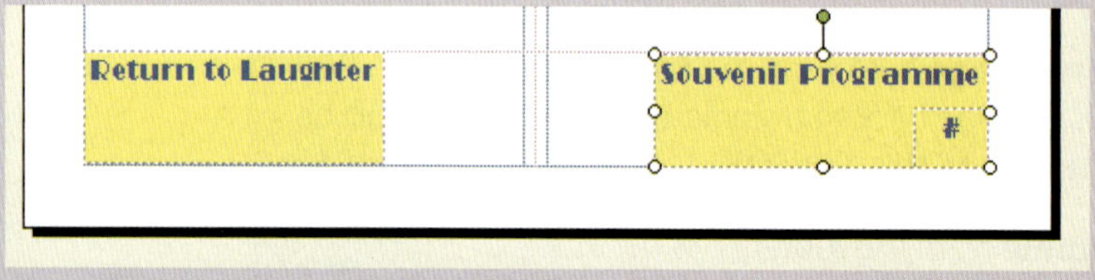

Figure 9.14: *The footer as two text frames.*

You now need to fill in the space between these boxes with yellow. You can do this by creating another, empty text frame between the two. This will be easier to do if you set up the frame to lock onto existing objects (the existing text frames) as well as onto the guidelines.

- Click the **Arrange** menu and choose **Snap** and **To Objects**.

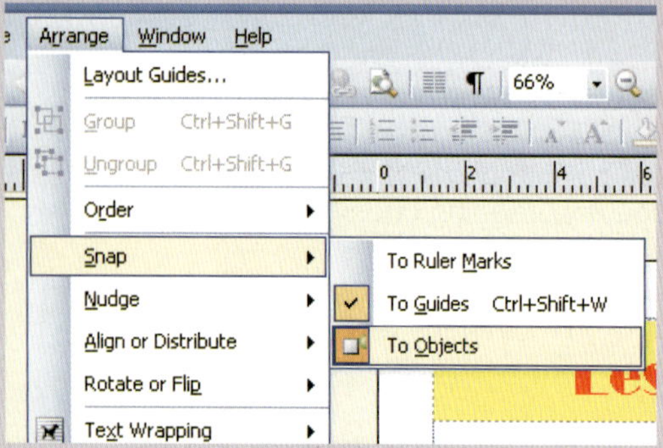

Figure 9.15: *Snap to objects as well as to guide frames.*

- Now use the **Text Box** tool to drag out another frame to fit between the two existing ones. Fill this with yellow to match these.

- Use **Arrange** → **Snap** to remove the snap **To Objects**, as this is not normally needed.
- Your footer should now look just the same as it did before. To see the effect of your changes click the **Change Single-Page/Two-Page** button on the **Edit Master Pages** toolbar again to convert your master page back to a two-page master.
- Click the **Close Master View** button on the **Edit Master Pages** toolbar.

At the moment your publication has only one page, so you cannot see the effect of your master pages.

- Click **Insert** on the menu bar and choose **Page...**.
- Choose **7** new pages, to bring your publication up to its required eight pages.

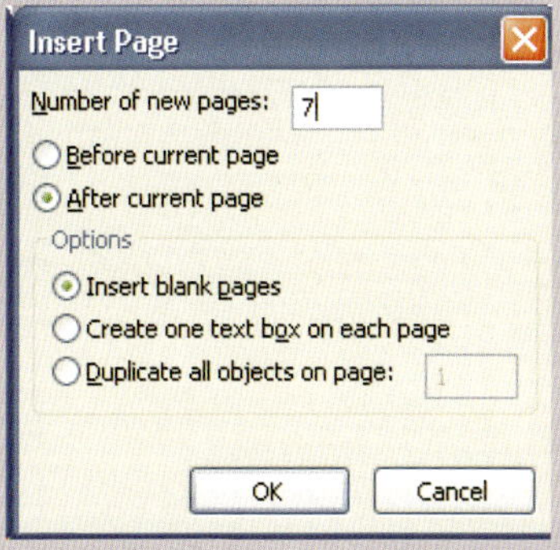

Figure 9.16: *Inserting seven new pages.*

You should now see that you have eight pages showing at the bottom of the working window. Click any of these to see them.

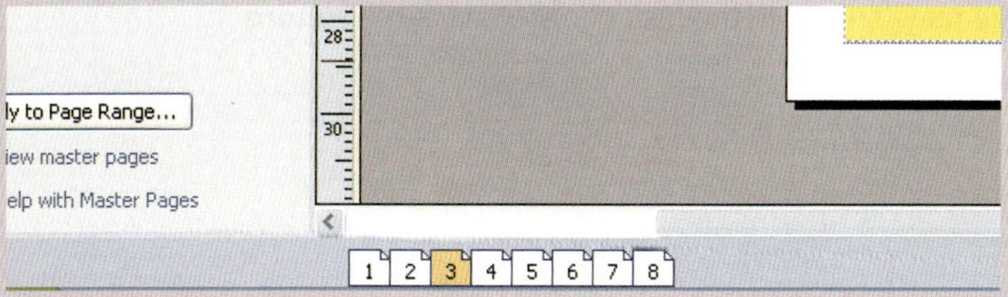

Figure 9.17: *The pages of your publication can be accessed from the bottom of the window.*

If you prefer to see facing pages together, use the **View** menu and choose **Two Page Spread**.

- Save your publication.

Ignoring the master page

Your publication now has eight pages, each one based on the master page you have created. It is possible to create more master pages and choose on which master page to base each page of your publication.

It is very common, as in our case, to want the front page to be of a different design. One way of dealing with this is to set Publisher to ignore the master page for the front page, so that you can create what you want from a completely blank page.

To set a page up in this way, make sure that the page you want to change is showing, then use the drop-down menu at the top of the task pane to change to **Apply Master Page**.

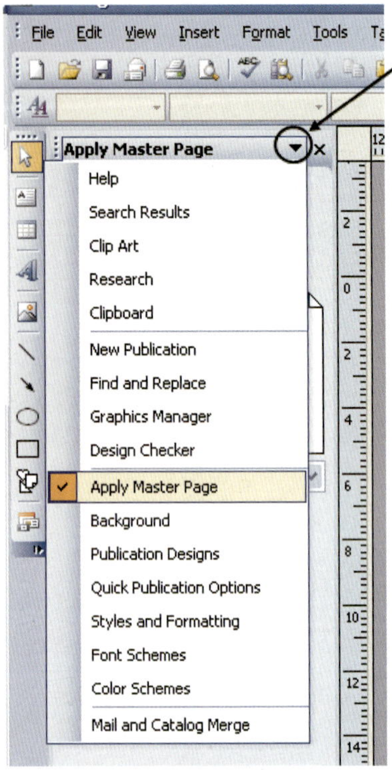

Figure 9.18: *Changing the task pane.*

Use the drop-down menu underneath the page shown in the task pane to select the **Ignore Master** option.

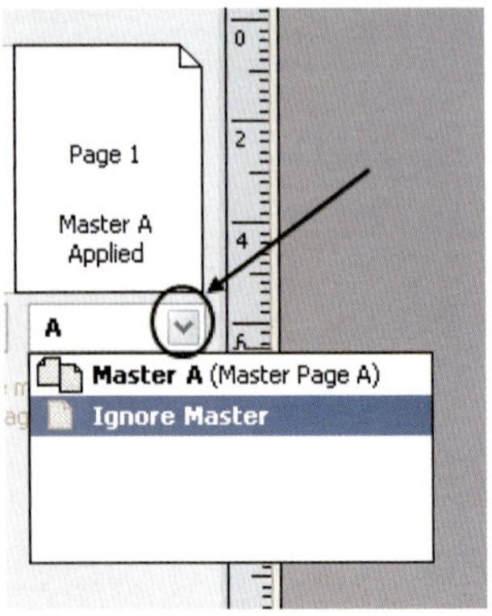

Figure 9.19: *Setting Page 1 to ignore the master page.*

Activity 3: Ignoring the master page...

In this activity you will set the first page of your publication to ignore the master page.

- Load the publication you saved at the end of Activity 2.
- The task pane will show the **Quick Publication Options**. Click the drop-down arrow next to this to choose **Apply Master Page**.

You should see Page 1 is shown set to **Master A Applied**.

- Click the drop-down menu below this. Choose **Ignore Master**.
- Click all the different pages in your publication, and you should now see that page 1 is blank, but all the other pages remain based on the master page you set in Activity 2.
- Save your publication.

Creating the pages of a publication

Frames

The main content of all publications is added by creating **frames** on the pages using one of the frame creation tools on the toolbar that is usually at the left of the Publisher window. These might be:

- text frames
- graphic frames.

Text and graphics can then be added to the relevant frames.

Text might be typed in, as on a word processor, or copied and pasted from another document. Alternatively you can use **Insert** → **Text File...** to import a complete word-processed file. In professional publications most text will be typed using a word processor, then imported into the DTP package, as word processors have more facilities that allow easy editing of text.

When you create a graphic frame in Microsoft Publisher you can choose to add a graphic from clip art, a file or a scanner/camera.

Microsoft Publisher also allows you to create WordArt frames, which are a special type of graphic frame that automatically create graphical text.

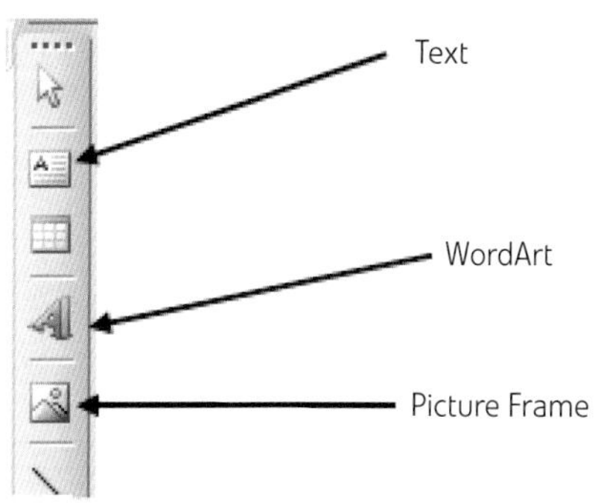

Figure 9.20: *Frame creation tools in Publisher.*

You should always try to use the layout guides to help you position frames. When moving frames on the page you will sometimes find it useful to use the **Arrange** → **Snap** → **To Objects** option to help get frames completely in line with each other.

Linking text frames

If you have a large amount of text it is likely to extend over more than one frame. You can deal with this very easily by **linking** frames together so that the software will automatically move to the second (or subsequent) frame once the first one is full of text.

To link two frames together, first create the two text frames, then click inside the first one and click the **Create Text Box Link** button on the toolbar.

Move your pointer over the second text frame and click inside it.

> **TIP**
>
> When you are importing text that is too large to fit into a single frame, Publisher will offer to create new frames for you. It is usually better to say 'no' to this, then create and link your own frames, as Publisher will rarely create new frames where you want them to be!

Hyphenation

Because a lot of DTP text is in columns, which can be quite narrow, it is common for DTP software to automatically hyphenate long words, to allow more words to fit on each line. If you don't like this you can change the hyphenation options by clicking on the **Tools** menu and choosing **Language** → **Hyphenation...**.

Widows, orphans and other problems to avoid

In DTP work you often need to move frames around the page until you get the best effect. When doing this there are a number of possible problems you need to avoid:

- You should never leave just one line from a paragraph at the bottom of a column or above a picture. This is called a **widow**. If necessary, move the whole paragraph to the next column or rearrange the frames in a different way so that this doesn't happen.
- Similarly, you should never allow just the last line of a paragraph (an **orphan**) to overflow on its own to a new column or below a picture.
- Never separate a title from the text it belongs to.
- Always check that all of your text is displayed. It is easy to make changes that mean that you have too much text to fit into the frame(s). If this happens you will see the **text overflow indicator** at the bottom of the frame when you click in it. If your text does overflow you will need to edit your text to make it shorter, make your text frame bigger, or create a new text frame and link your full frame to it.

Key terms

Widow

A single line of text (or sometimes just one or two words) which is separated from a paragraph and left at the top of a page or column, or below a picture or text feature. A widow is usually the last line of a paragraph.

Orphan

A single line of text which is separated from a paragraph and left at the bottom of a page or column, or above a picture or text feature. An orphan is usually the first line of a paragraph.

When you set or modify a style, there are two tabs on the **paragraph** option. In Chapter 2 we only looked at the **Indents and Spacing** tab because this contains all the settings that are required for success in this unit. However, the other tab, **Line and Paragraph Breaks**, can help prevent widows, orphans and abandoned headings.

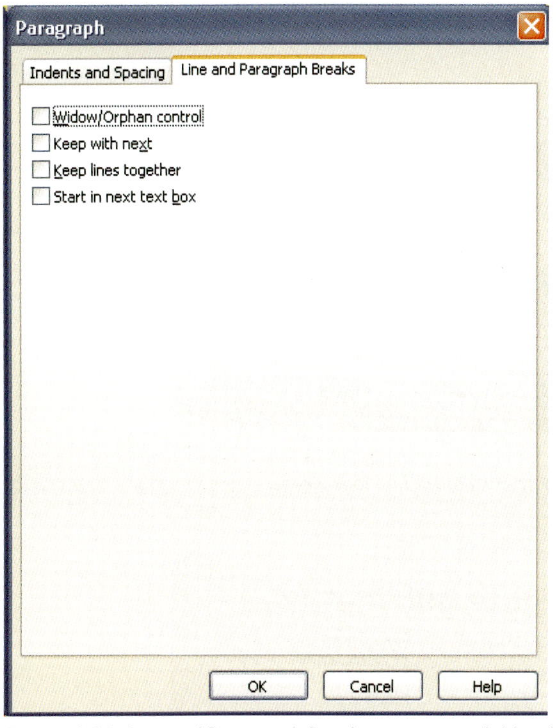

***Figure 9.21:** Line and Paragraph Breaks options available when setting styles.*

- Check the **Widow/Orphan control** box for styles such as **Body text**, which will be used for paragraphs of writing that might move onto more than one column or page.
- Check the **Keep with next** box for styles such as **Main Heading** and **Sub Heading**, where you will never want the text to be the last thing at the bottom of a column or page.
- It is also advisable to check the **Keep lines together** box for headings. Although you would expect most, if not all, headings to be single lines, occasionally one might be more than a line long, especially if you are working on narrow columns, and you certainly don't want a heading broken between columns or pages.

Graphic frames

The most common things you will need to do to graphic frames is **resize** and **crop** them so that they can fit into the space available. This is done in exactly the same way as in other programs such as word processors and web design packages.

Remember that your aim is to present information as clearly as possible so you must try to remember the following:

- Avoid increasing the size of small bitmap images (these are the ones made up of tiny blocks called **pixels**) so much that they lose their smoothness. No matter how much you might want to use a particular picture at a particular size, if it doesn't look good at the size you want it, choose something else!

- Don't make pictures so small that they cannot be clearly seen. If you really want the picture then make room for it, perhaps by editing some text or removing another graphic.
- Never distort photographs by stretching them. This is a common error, often resulting in pictures of tall and thin or short and fat people and objects, which look little like the real thing!

Figure 9.22: *Not a pretty sight at the best of times, but stretching photos will make him look worse!*

Activity 4: Creating the front page of your publication...

In this activity you will create the front page for the Les and Des programme by:

- setting a second master page
- adding text frames
- adding graphic frames
- adding WordArt frames
- setting graphics as a watermark.

➔ Load the publication you saved at the end of Activity 3.

➔ The publication will load with Page 1 showing. This is the page you are going to create.

Refer to the plan for this page in Figure 7.2. This shows the page divided horizontally 1/3 to 2/3. It would be helpful to have layout guides here. This can be done by creating a second master page.

➔ Choose **View** → **Master Pages** then click on the **New Master Page** button [New Master Page...] at the bottom of the task pane. There is no need to change the suggested name, but uncheck the **Two-page master** box before clicking **OK**.

➔ Choose **Arrange** → **Layout Guides...** and set the margins to **1.5cm**, then set the grid guides to **3** columns and **12** rows, with **0cm** space between any of these.

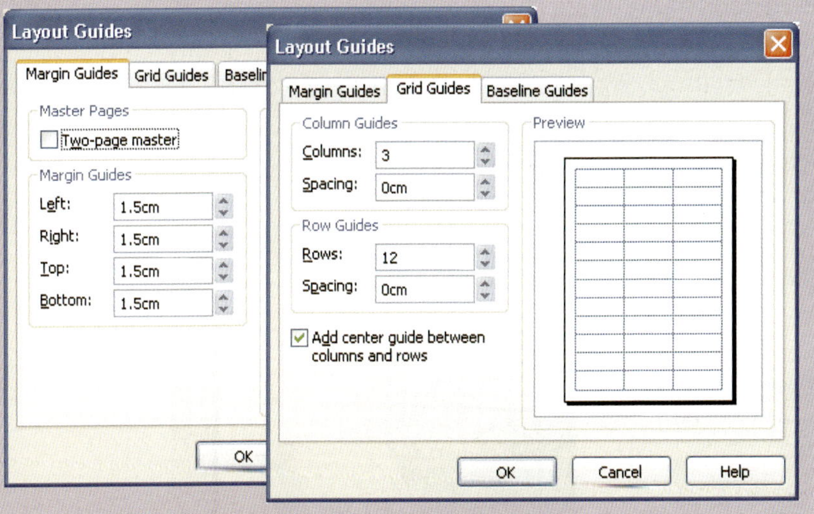

***Figure 9.23:** Setting the layout guides for the new master page.*

- Click **View publication pages** at the bottom of the task pane and use the drop-down menu underneath Page 1 to choose your new **Master B**.
- In the top right-hand corner of the page, create a text frame that goes across the first column and the first four rows.
- Choose the **LD Header** style, which is the nearest to the style required here. Type the word **Les**, then press **Enter**.
- Choose the **LD Header** style again, then type the word **and**, then add the word **Des** underneath in the same way.
- Increase the size of **Les** and **Des** to **60** point but leave the **and** at the original 36 point size.
- Fill the frame with yellow.
- Create a text frame along the whole width of the bottom row. Use the **LD Footer** style to type the text **SOUVENIR PROGRAMME**, then centre the text and increase the size to **36** point.
- Fill this frame with yellow.
- You should notice that the text is not exactly centred vertically – it is nearer the top of the frame than the bottom. You can change this by using **Format** → **Paragraph** and setting the **Line Spacing** in the **Before Paragraph** box. You can experiment with different numbers here, but you should find that 9 pt is about right.
- Create some graphic frames in the remaining space in the left-hand column and import some photographs of Les and Des from the **OCR Level 2 Nationals Unit 5 Student Resources** → **Photos** → **Les and Des** folder. Crop, resize and move these until you have filled the space appropriately. You will find the **Arrange** → **Snap** → **To Objects** option useful here.

The plan in Figure 7.2 shows photographs of audiences across the right-hand two columns.

- At the top of the page create a graphic frame across these two columns, and choose a photograph from the **OCR Level 2 Nationals Unit 5 Student Resources → Photos → Crowds** folder. Add two more crowd photographs then crop and move the three crowd photographs until they fill the space.
- Right-click the top crowd photograph and choose **Format picture...**. Click the **Picture** tab and set the **Color** option to **Washout** using the drop-down box. This will convert the photograph into a watermark.

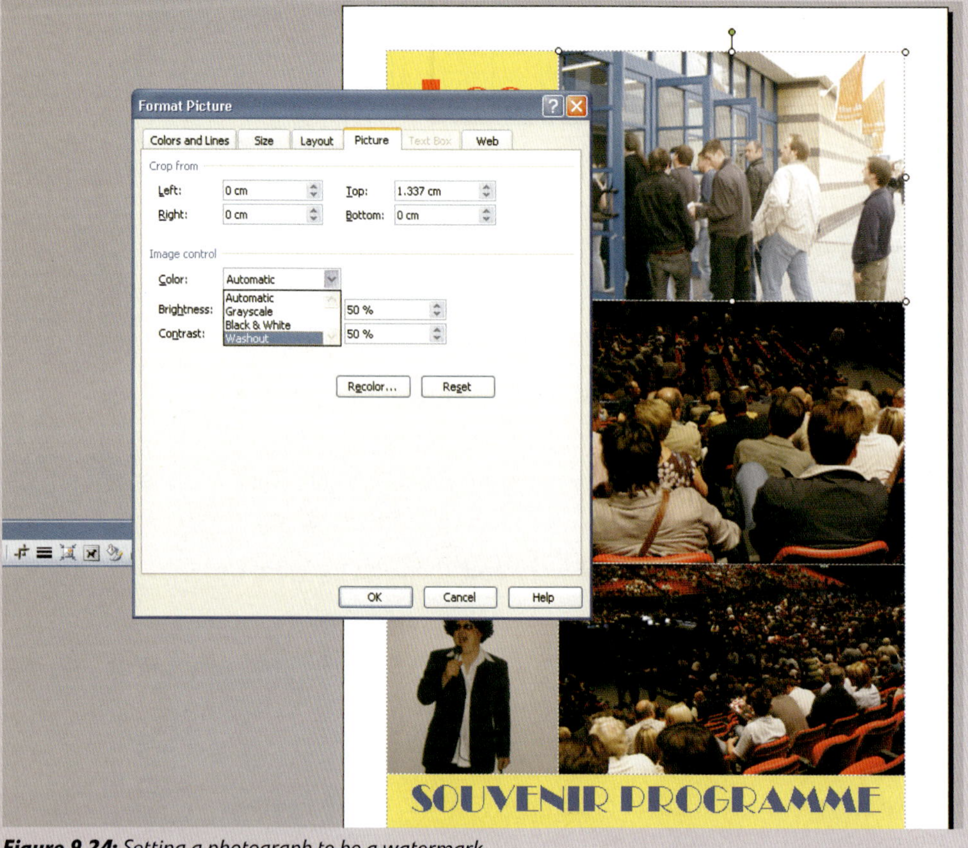

Figure 9.24: *Setting a photograph to be a watermark.*

- Convert the remaining two crowd photographs to watermarks in the same way.
- Choose the **WordArt** tool to add the text to the right-hand side. There is no option that looks like the planned text, so choose the second option on the top row, as this shows the sort of solid text we need.
- Type the word **Return**, change the font to **Broadway** and click **OK**.

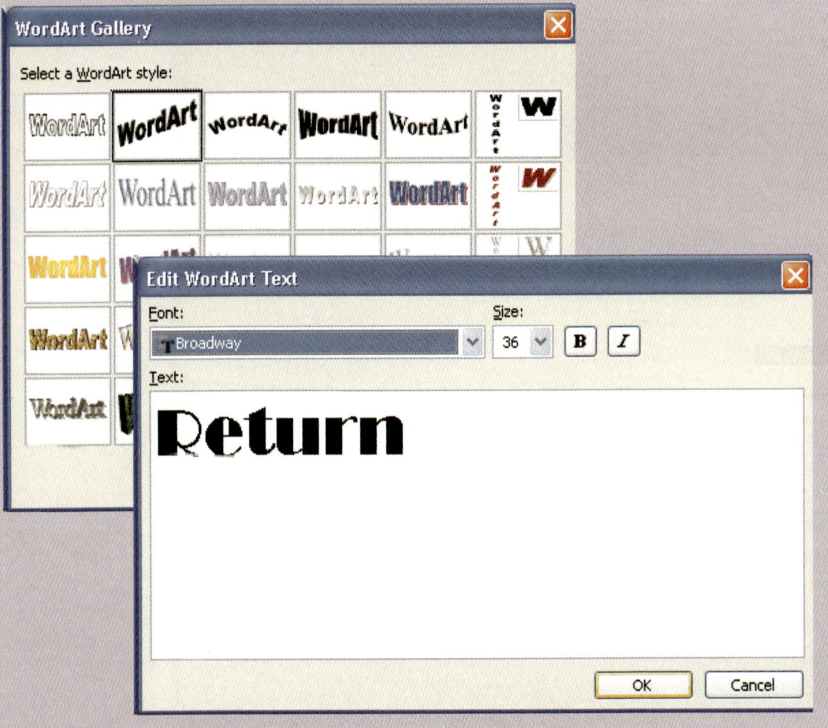

Figure 9.25: *Using WordArt*

- The plan shows the text slanting down to the right. Do this using the **WordArt Shape** tool on the WordArt toolbar. Click this and choose the **Slant Down** shape.

Figure 9.26: *Changing the WordArt shape.*

- Now that the text is the correct shape you need to change its colour to **red**. Do this by choosing **Format WordArt** from the WordArt toolbar, then selecting the red fill colour on the **Colors and Lines** tab.

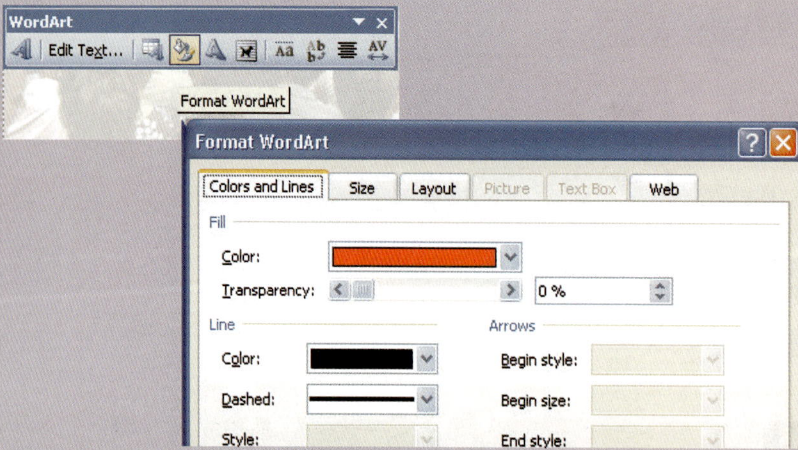

Figure 9.27: *Changing the text colour of WordArt.*

- Add a shadow using the **Shadow Style** tool on the formatting toolbar at the top of the window. Choose the style you think fits best.
- Change the shadow colour to yellow, as on the plan, by choosing **Shadow Settings** from the **Shadow Style** tool. You can experiment moving the shadow here too.

Figure 9.28: *Shadow settings.*

- Now you have the word 'Return' you could repeat the process to create WordArt frames for 'to' and 'Laughter'. However, the simplest method is to copy and paste the 'Return' frame twice, then double click on each to change the text to 'to' and 'Laughter'.
- Resize and move the three WordArt frames as required.
- When you are happy with your front page, save your file.

Activity 5: Adding text and graphics...

In this activity you will complete pages 2 and 3 of your programme by:

- adding text and graphics frames
- linking frames
- importing text
- applying formatting
- setting widow and orphan control
- adding headings
- importing graphics.

→ Load the publication you saved at the end of Activity 4.

→ Create two text frames on Page 2 of your publication, one for each column identified by the blue layout guides.

→ Click in the first frame, then click the **Create Text Box Link** button on the toolbar. Move down and click in the second frame to link the two frames.

→ Click again in the first frame, then choose **Insert** → **Text file...**. Select the file **Les Gets Bio** from the **OCR Level 2 Nationals Unit 5 Student Resources** → **Articles** folder. This inserts text into the frame, which will automatically overflow into your second frame.

→ Select all of this text using **Ctrl + A**, then use **Format** → **Styles and Formatting** to choose **Body Text** style for this text.

→ Click the menu arrow next to the **Body text** style in the **Styles and Formatting** window to **Modify...** the style. Choose the **Paragraph...** option, then select the **Line and Paragraph Breaks** tab and tick the **Widow/Orphan control** box.

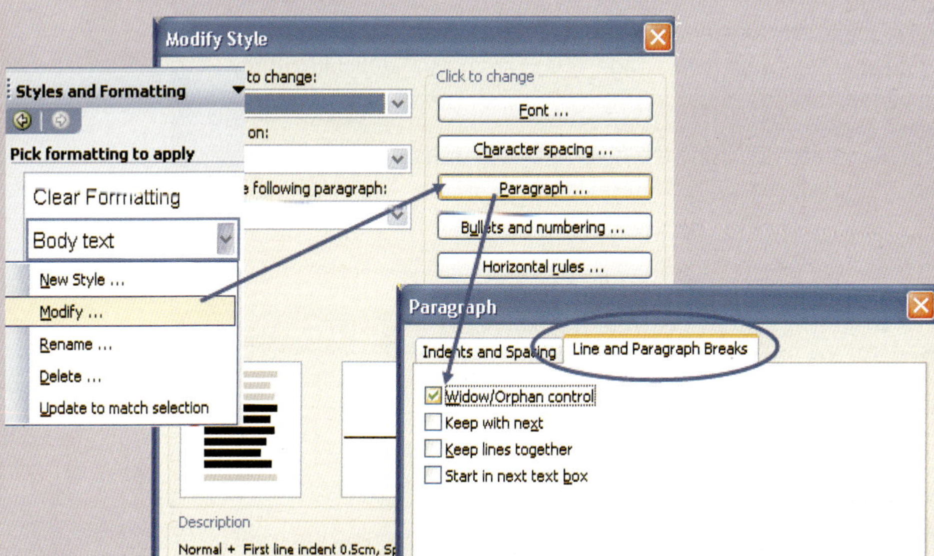

Figure 9.29: *Setting Widow and orphan control for the* ***Body Text*** *style.*

- Click the menu arrow next to the **Main Heading** style in the **Styles and Formatting** window to **Modify...** the style. Choose the **Paragraph...** option, then select the **Line and Paragraph Breaks** tab and tick both **Keep with next** and **Keep lines together** boxes.
- Modify the **Sub Heading** style in the same way, to prevent sub-headings being split or separated from the following text.
- Insert a new line at the top of the first frame and choose the **Main Heading** style. Type in an appropriate heading for this article.
- Read through the text and split it up by adding any sub-headings you want, using the **Sub Heading** style.
- Add a suitable photograph of Les from the **OCR Level 2 Nationals Unit 5 Student Resources → Photos → Les and Des** folder. Crop, resize and move this as appropriate.

You should have a little space for a quote somewhere on the page. If not, you will need to edit some of the text to make it shorter.

- Create a small text frame for your quote. You can put this wherever you think it will look best.
- Open up the Word document **quotes.doc** from the **OCR Level 2 Nationals Unit 5 Student Resources → Quotes** folder. This contains a selection of quotes that you can use in this publication. Copy and paste one quote into your new text box. Choose one that looks about the right length for the amount of space you have available.
- Use **Ctrl + A** to select all the text in the quote, then choose the **Quotes** style.
- Fill the frame with blue.
- Check your page and make any further adjustments that are necessary. If you have too much space, add another quote to the page. If you are having difficulty fitting everything on the page, make the photograph smaller or delete some of the text.
- Complete Page 3 in the same way, using the text file **Des Trunks Bio** and a suitable photograph of Des.
- Save your publication.

Activity 6: Completing your publication...

In this activity you will:

- add text and graphics to the remaining five pages of your programme
- rearrange all pages to complete the publication.

In this activity you can be more creative. You need to complete the remaining pages of your publication, choosing suitable text and graphics and adding your own headings and sub-headings as appropriate.

You can choose to use files supplied in the OCR Level 2 Nationals Unit 5 Student Resources folder but you can also find and create resources of your own, to make your programme more individual, and perhaps more relevant to your own local area.

You might search on the Internet for text and graphics about concert venues in the North of England or you might like to take some photographs of venues in your own local area.

Additional adverts could be obtained by scanning them in from local newspapers and magazines. Alternatively you could create adverts of your own.

You can edit any of the provided files. For example, you might wish to change some of the concert venues to match your photographs or to ensure your local area features in the Les and Des comeback tour!

You should be able to use the adverts and quotes to help you fill each page well. Remember that the original plan suggested that the quotes would be 'scattered in different places throughout the publication'.

Try to create an original programme that still meets the requirements set out in the practice assignment given in Chapter 7.

Although you should keep to the main styles outlined in the design, there is no need to stick rigidly to exactly the same format for each page. For example, there might be at least one page where two columns are not appropriate and you want to put all your text in a single column. That is perfectly acceptable. Remember what you learnt when you looked at existing programmes. Try to keep a recognisable house style throughout your publication without making every page look exactly the same.

Don't overfill your pages. You should have seen from your research in Chapter 7 that pages are much more attractive and easy to read if they are not cluttered and crammed full. A little white space between items makes the pages less intimidating to the reader. Additionally, you are going to add extra graphic items in Chapter 10, so you will need to leave some space for these!

Save your completed publication.

Error checking

When creating any document it is important that you check it thoroughly for errors at every stage. You should already be familiar with two types of check:

- Spell/grammar check – performed by the software.
- Visual check – carried out by yourself or someone else, reading through the document carefully.

Most DTP software includes a spellcheck feature but not a grammar checker. If you wish to check text using a grammar checker you need to check it in a word processor first, then import it into your DTP software.

Publisher offers one further type of check, which is very useful and should always be carried out. This is called the **Design checker** and it can be found on the **Tools** menu. When you run the Design Checker it will check through your whole publication for possible errors such as:

- text frames that have text overflow
- graphics that have been stretched out of their original proportion

- objects that are not visible, because they have been covered up by others
- objects that are partially off the page or in the area at the edge of a page that will not print.

As with a grammar checker, these will not always be errors. However, the checker highlights *potential* problems, so that you can look at these more carefully and make your own decision.

Errors are displayed in the task pane to the left of your screen. For each error you are given a choice from a drop-down menu.

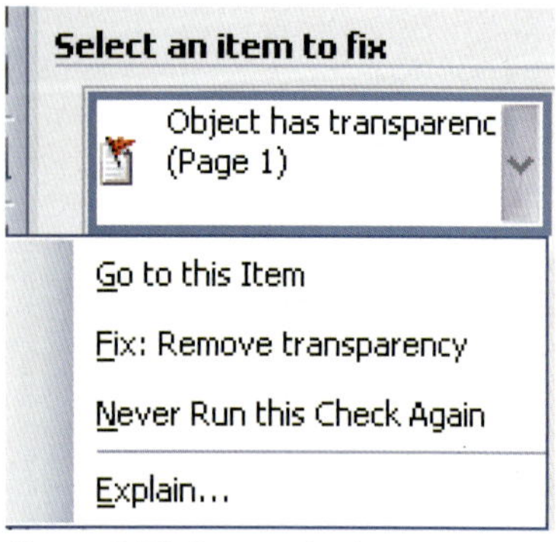

Figure 9.30: *Design checker options.*

- **Go to this Item**: This allows you to see where in your publication the possible error is. You do not need to use the drop-down menu for this, as this will be done if you just click the error message.
- **Fix**: This is not always available, but sometimes it is possible to fix the 'problem' automatically. If a picture has been stretched out of proportion then this might be a useful option. It can also be quite useful to choose this option to see the effect. If you don't like it you can always use the **undo** button to reverse the 'fix'. Remember that the Design Checker is just following rules – it is not always right!
- **Never Run this Check Again**: Be very careful before choosing this option. This does not just ignore the current frame, but will prevent the Design Checker from finding any similar potential problems anywhere else. Only choose this option if you are absolutely sure that you do not want this sort of error message to be displayed again. If you do choose this option by mistake you can reinstate the check using the **Design Checker Options** link at the bottom of the task pane.
- **Explain...**: This can be a useful option at first. Use it to help you understand why the system thinks that there may be an error.

Activity 7: Checking your publication...

In this activity you will:

- use the spellchecker
- use the design checker.

➔ Load the publication you saved at the end of Activity 5.

➔ Spell check your text in the same way as you would a word-processed document. The only difference is that Publisher checks each 'story' separately, i.e. each set of linked text frames. When asked if you want to check the next story, answer **Yes**.

➔ Choose **Tools** from the menu bar and choose **Design Checker...**.

You will now see a series of queries in the task pane on the left. If no queries appear the Design Checker has not identified any problems with your document.

- Click the first query. The relevant frame will be highlighted so that you can see what you want to do.
- Click the drop-down menu arrow to the right of the first query. This will show you your options. If you are not sure what to do, choose the **Explain...** option. If you are still not sure, choose **Fix** if it is available, to see what difference this makes. You can then choose whether or not to keep this amendment or **undo** it and either ignore the error message or make a change yourself.
- Check all the queries in this way.
- Finish by clicking on the **Close Design Checker** button at the bottom of the task pane.
- Save your publication.

Portfolio builder

For your own portfolio you will need to create your own eight-page publication by, for example:

- setting master page(s)
- setting margins
- setting layout guides
- creating frames, linking them where necessary
- adding new text from the keyboard – this may be just headings or it may be longer pieces
- importing text
- formatting text using the styles created in Chapter 8
- adding any additional formatting required by particular items
- importing graphics from file/camera/scanner/Internet/clip art
- resizing and cropping graphics
- using the snap to objects option, where appropriate
- adding and editing WordArt, if appropriate
- spell checking
- using the Design Checker.

You do not need to use all of these features. Indeed, some might not be appropriate for your particular publication. However, to gain the higher levels you will be expected to use more features than are required for a **Pass** grade.

The main evidence for this assessment objective will be the completed publication. However, the use of many of the features listed above cannot be seen just by looking at the completed document, so you should gather additional evidence to clearly show the features you have used. This will most effectively be by a few key screenshots, with short annotations. You are **not** expected to give detailed descriptions of everything you do to create your publication.

CHAPTER 10

Assessment Objective 4

Use Drawing Tools Included with DTP Software to Create Basic Shapes

Overview:

In this chapter you will look at Microsoft Publisher's range of graphical tools that can be used to enhance your publication. You will first consider further techniques that can be used to make small amounts of text stand out, then you will look at the drawing tools.

In order to complete the activities in this chapter you will need access to a number of additional files. These files are contained in the Unit 5 Student Resources zip file which can be downloaded from the OCR nationals in ICT (Units 3 & 5) Student Resources page on the Payne-Gallway website: www.payne-gallway.co.uk

How this assessment objective will be assessed...

You will be assessed on the following aspects of your work:

- Your final publication will show most of the features you have used, and the range and appropriateness of tools used will be assessed.
- Screenshots will be used to demonstrate any features and techniques used that cannot be clearly seen from the final publication.

Skills to use...

For this objective you will need to show a mastery of the basic graphics tools available from within the DTP program you are using, for example:

- a range of text styles and effects, including reverse text and artistic text (known in Publisher as WordArt)
- a range of 2-D shapes
- tools to cut and paste, copy and crop
- monochrome and colour fill and shading
- lines of different styles and colour
- layering items to create a clear graphic
- grouping.

The use of WordArt is included in this Assessment Objective, but this has already been covered in Chapter 9. You have probably also cropped images when you inserted graphics in Chapter 9.

Although this chapter will concentrate solely on the tools that are available within Publisher, you may also choose to demonstrate your graphical skills by using specialist graphics software and including the resulting graphics in your final publication.

How to achieve...

Pass requirements

P1 You will use a limited range of drawing facilities to produce shapes.

P2 You will demonstrate some limited use of layering.

Merit requirements

M1 You will use the majority of tools listed in the **Skills to use** section above, including layering and grouping, to produce accurate drawings.

M2 You will have combined different shapes to create a more complex whole.

Distinction requirements

D1 You will consistently use the full range of tools listed in the **Skills to use** section above to create complex shapes which clearly suit the needs of the brief and the intended audience.

D2 You will include lines and borders in the completed document.

Text styles

You are already familiar with the use of different font faces, styles and emphasis. There are some other effects that are worth looking at and considering:

- Outline
- Emboss
- Shadow
- Engrave.

To see these effects, type a piece of text in a text frame in Publisher, highlight it and then select **Format** from the menu bar and choose **Font...**. Here you can experiment with the different effects that are available. The results of some may not be very obvious with small text, so it is best to work with a large font size. You might also see some effects more clearly if you change the colour of the text and/or the background.

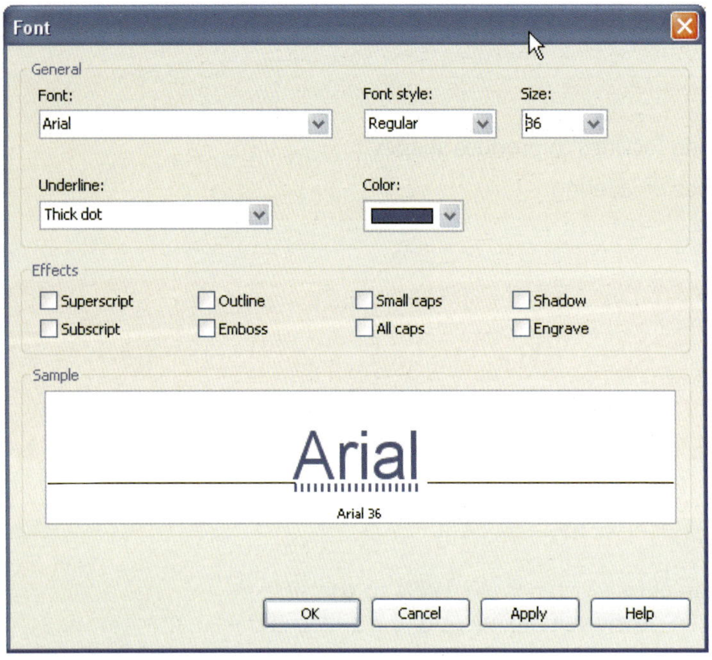

Figure 10.1: *Text effects available from the* ***Format*** *→* ***Font...*** *menu option.*

Reverse text

One effect that you may often see on professional DTP documents is reverse text, sometimes called **knockout text**, where white text on a black background is used in contrast to the normal black text on a white background. This is particularly common for titles or other small items of text that need to stand out clearly. If you have access to any documents from OCR for this qualification, for example the specification for the units or any of the sample assignments, you will see that this effect is part of the OCR house style.

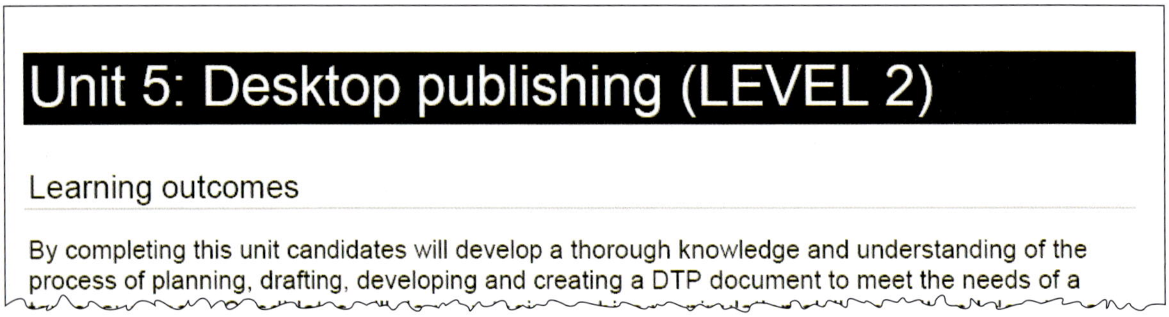

Figure 10.2: *An example use of reverse text.*

Although in a black and white document reverse text is white text on a black background, in a coloured document it can use other colours, with light text on a dark background. This would usually be a reversal of the main colours on the document. For example, if the main colour scheme uses red text on a white background then reverse text would be white text on a red background.

The best way to achieve reverse text for a title in Microsoft Publisher is to create a text box for your title, fill it with black (or another dark colour) and then choose white (or a light) font colour before typing in your text. You may then need to adjust the size of your text and text box. Do not forget that you can use **Format → Paragraph...** to increase the space before the paragraph, to move the text down the box if required. Ideally your text will be fairly central vertically in the box, as in the example in Figure 10.2. If you want to use this style in a number of places in a document the best method is to create and format the first text box, then, when you have got it looking just as you want, copy and paste it to other places in your document as required so that you simply have to edit the text, and the format will be identical.

Use reverse text very sparingly – while it can make particular items stand out, it is generally considered to be more difficult to read. In the plan for the Les and Des programme the quotes are planned as yellow text on a blue background – this is in fact reverse text as it is a reversal of the colour scheme for the footers. You might like to experiment with your publication to see if this creates any readability problems. However, it is acceptable for small amounts of text such as the quotes.

Drop capitals

Another common text effect is the dropped capital. You might see this used for the first paragraph in a chapter or article.

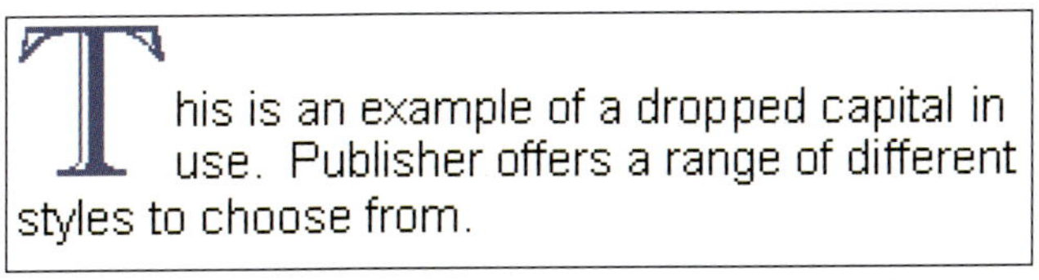

Figure 10.3: *A dropped capital can be used to highlight the beginning of an article.*

To create a dropped capital, first type in your paragraph as normal. Then, with the cursor anywhere in the paragraph, click **Format** on the menu bar and choose **Drop Cap...**. Choose the style you like and click **OK**.

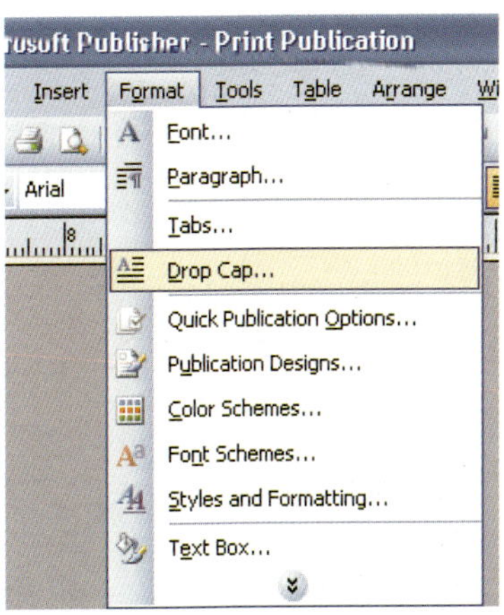

Figure 10.4: *Choosing the* ***Drop Cap...*** *option.*

Activity 1: Adding text effects...

In this activity you will add further text effects to your publication.

- Load the publication you saved at the end of your work in Chapter 9.
- Move to Page 2, where you are going to change the title **Les Gets** into reverse text.
- Select the title **Les Gets** at the top of the page and **cut** it.
- Adjust the size of the text frame by moving the top handle down, until there is space to create a new frame for the title. You should make sure that the column breaks in the same place as before.

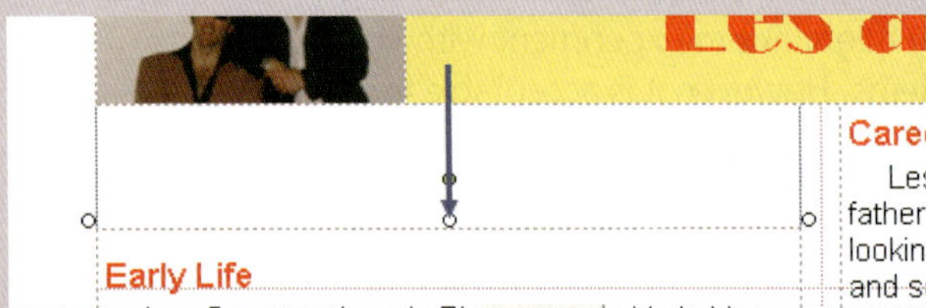

Figure 10.5: *Adjust the size of the text frame to make room for the heading in a new frame.*

- Use the **Text box** tool from the left-hand toolbar to create a new text frame above the original one. **Paste** the text into it.
- **Centre** the title in the new text box.
- Select the title and change the text colour to **white** and the background to **red**.
- Use the **Format → Paragraph...** option to adjust the spacing above and below the line of text, to make it sit exactly centrally in the box. It is unlikely you'll get this right at the first attempt – take a little time to experiment with different amounts of spacing until you think it is exactly right. You might find it useful to zoom in to see your work at 200% or 400% for this.

Figure 10.6: *The title converted to reverse text.*

In order to maintain a consistent style for facing pages you now need to change the heading for Page 3 too.

- Copy and paste the new frame you have just made. For now, don't worry where to put it – move it to the work area above Page 3.
- Now **cut** the main heading from Page 3 and adjust the size of the main text frame as before.

- Move the copied red frame into place at the top of the page, then delete the text and **paste** the required title in place. If at first you don't see the text, this is likely to be because the text has kept its original format (red), so that it can't be seen on the red background. Click the format option box at the bottom right-hand corner and choose **Keep text only**. Because you copied the frame from Page 2 you no longer need to change any other formatting.
- Choose another page of your publication, where you can use a dropped capital to emphasise the first paragraph. Click in the paragraph and choose **Format → Drop Cap...**. Experiment with the available options until you find one you think is suitable.
- You may wish to delete any sub-heading before this paragraph as the dropped capital is probably emphasis enough. You will also have to look at the whole page to make sure that there is still room for all the text. If not, you may have to edit the text slightly, or reduce the size of a picture, in order to fit everything on the page.
- You may wish to create a dropped capital for the start of other pages/items too.
- Look at the options available from the **Format → Font...** menu. Have a look through your publication and see if there are any opportunities to use any of these features too.
- Save your publication, using a new name so that you have both versions available, to show the changes you have made.

Drawing shapes

If you need to create graphics for a publication you would normally produce these using a specialised graphics package and then import them into your DTP publication. However, it is possible to create simple shapes from within most DTP packages, which can save time if you want a simple line, box or outline. An added advantage of using these shapes is that you can easily add text to them without creating an extra text box.

Publisher has special tools for lines, arrows, ellipses (including circles) and rectangles (including squares), and a range of other shapes are available from **AutoShapes**, accessible from the **Objects** toolbar.

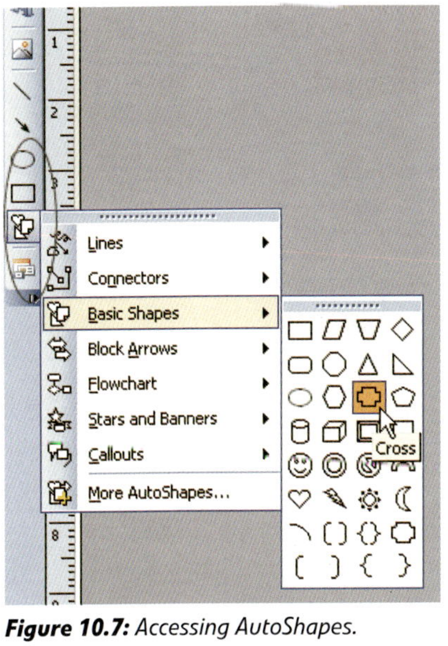

Figure 10.7: *Accessing AutoShapes.*

Again, the best way to see the range of shapes available is to experiment! Choose a tool/shape, then drag out the shape onto a document. You can then edit this using the handles, just like any other frame.

To add text to a shape, right click in the shape and choose **Add Text**.

Figure 10.8: *Text can be easily added to shapes.*

The basic colour, border, shadow and 3-D tools on the formatting toolbar can be used to format shapes in the same way as text frames and WordArt. All the usual text formatting tools can be used to format any text inside a shape, and margins can be moved using the ruler if needed.

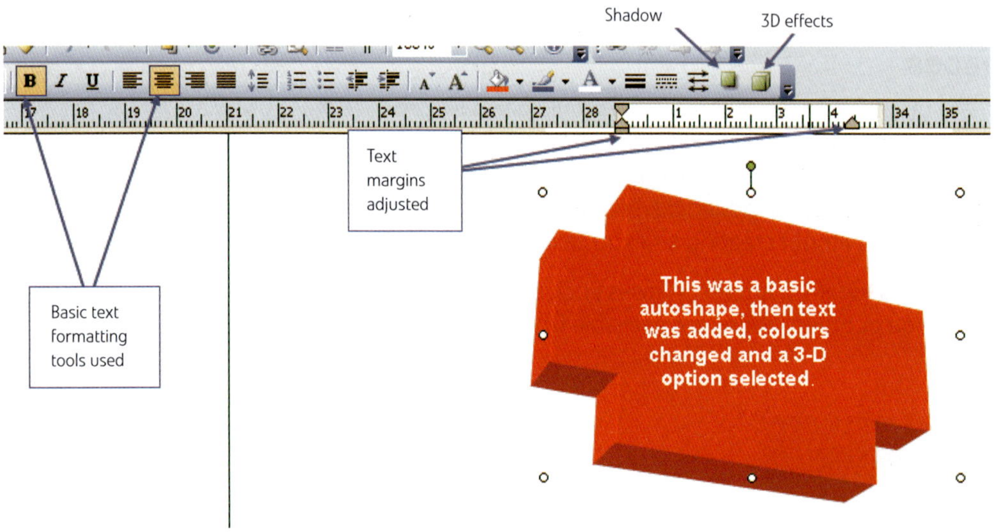

Figure 10.9: *Tools that can be used to edit basic shapes.*

Activity 2: Adding shapes...

In this activity you will:

- add a range of shapes to your publication
- add text to shapes
- change fill colours
- change line style and colour.

Load the publication you saved at the end of Activity 1.

You are free to experiment with your own ideas in this activity. Shapes will probably be most effective if you use them with small pieces of text. You might like to change some or all of the quotes to shapes. You could even go to the Master page and create a shape to put the page number in.

Try to add a variety of different shapes and experiment with a range of different styles, including fill colours, line styles/thicknesses, line colours, shading and 3-D effects.

Save your work using a different filename, so that you don't lose the original file.

If possible, look at the way other people are using shapes. Discuss ideas and see where you think they are most effective.

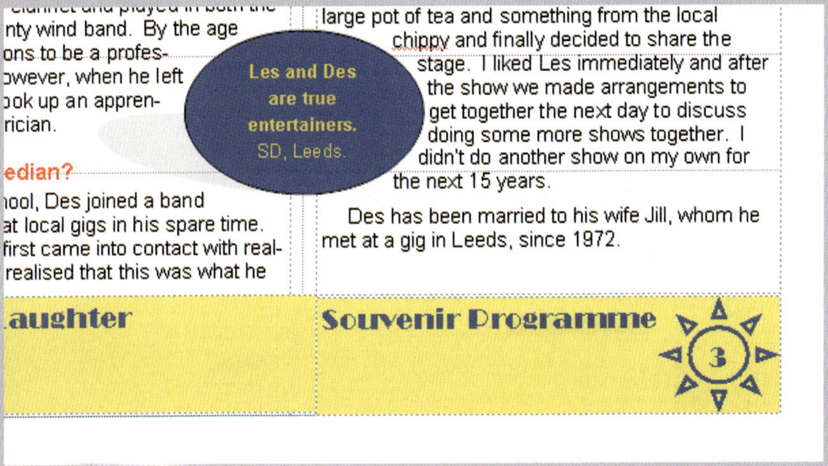

***Figure 10.10:** Shapes can be used to make quotes and page numbers more interesting.*

Fill effects

You have used the **Fill Color** tool to fill text frames and graphic objects with colour. This tool also gives you a choice of fill effects.

To see the effects that are available, click on the down arrow next to the **Fill Color** button on the formatting toolbar, then choose **Fill Effects...**.

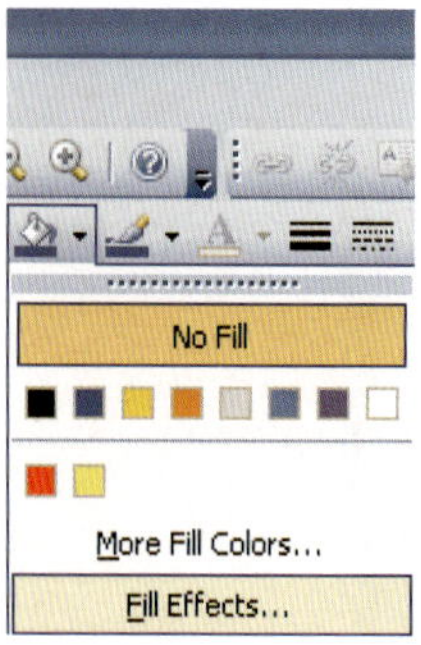

Figure 10.11: *Accessing the **Fill Effects...** menu.*

Again, the best way to find out about all the available options is to experiment. Draw a simple shape and try out various fill effect options. Some points to especially note are:

- if your publication is to be printed in black and white only, you should look at the options under the **Gradient** and **Pattern** tabs, choosing black and white as the two colours.

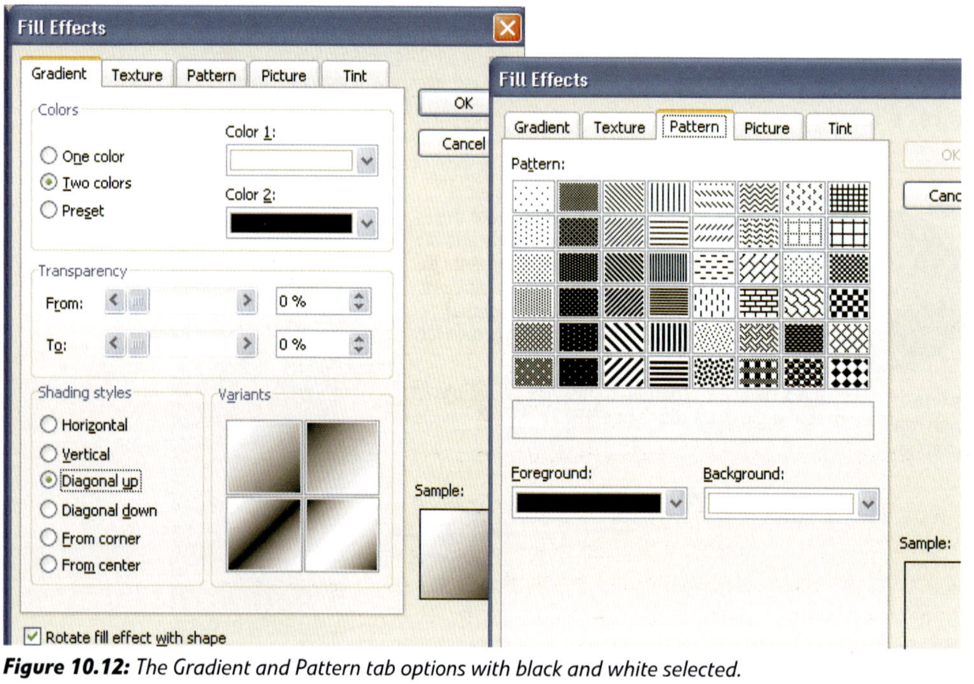

Figure 10.12: *The Gradient and Pattern tab options with black and white selected.*

- although the **Texture** tab options may look interesting, there is only a limited range to choose from, so you may not find a good use for any of them.
- if you choose the **Picture** tab you can choose any picture/photograph saved on your computer system. That means that you can fit some of the photographs into more interesting shapes if you wish. If you do use a photograph, make sure you tick the **Lock picture aspect ratio** box. This will adjust the shape proportions to fit the photograph, rather than stretching the photograph to match the shape. Remember that, since a photograph's purpose is usually to represent reality, you must almost never stretch one.

TIP

If the photograph you want to fill with is not the right shape, import it to the page and crop it, then right click and choose 'Save as picture'. You can then choose this new picture to fill with.

Figure 10.13: *Choosing a photo as a fill effect (with the* ***Lock picture aspect ratio*** *box ticked).*

- the **Tint** tab options are an easy way of accessing different shades of the same colour, which is useful if you are having your leaflet printed in a limited number of colours or if you want to keep to a particular colour scheme. The final effect is no different from choosing from the main colour options, but it is the easiest way of getting a range of related tints of a particular colour.

Activity 3: Fill effects...

In this activity you will:

- investigate a variety of fill effects
- change some frames/objects to gradient fill
- fill an object with a photograph.

➔ Load the publication you saved at the end of Activity 2.

➔ Draw a large oval shape in the working space outside your publication.

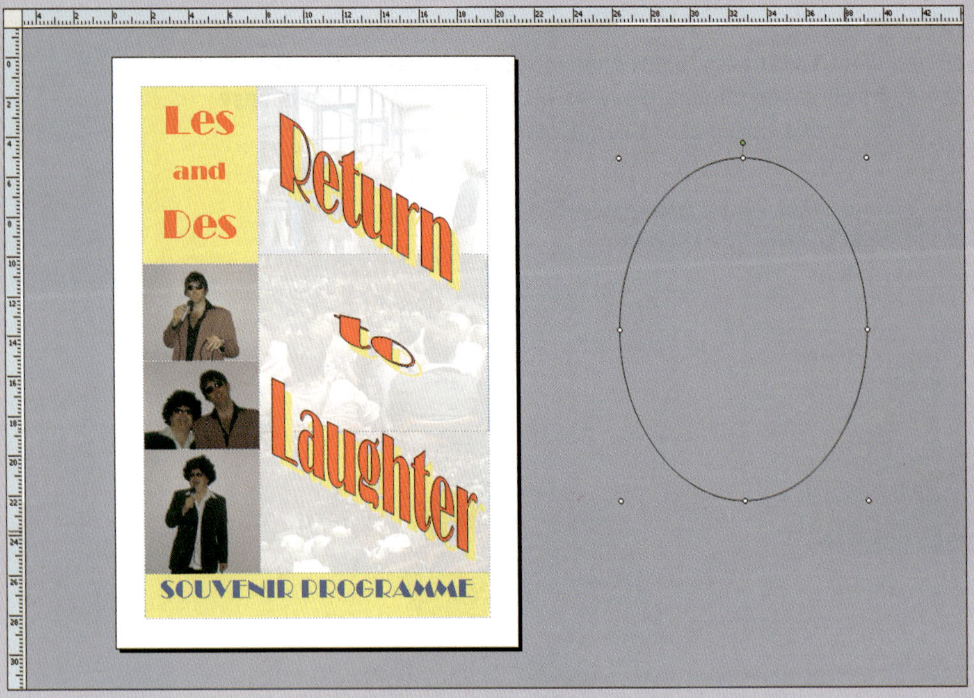

***Figure 10.14:** Drawing a large oval in the working area outside the page.*

- Click the down arrow next to the **Fill Color** button on the toolbar and choose **Fill Effects...**.
- Experiment with the different effects available.
  - Try out the **Gradient** tab options, trying **One colour** and **Two colours**, with the various **Shading styles**. Have a look at the **Preset** options too.
  - Try setting the **Transparency** options. You will need to move the filled shape over some of your completed page to see this effect.
  - Look at some of the options under **Texture** tab. Can you see any that you think might be useful to you?
  - Try out a few **Pattern** tab options, changing the **Background** and **Foreground** colours.
  - Look at the range of **tints** available by choosing a few different base colours.
  - Choose the **Picture** tab options and select one of the Les and Des photos from the **OCR Level 2 Nationals Unit 5 Student Resources** → **Photos** folder. Tick the **Lock picture aspect ratio** button before clicking **OK**.
- Look at the shapes you have already added to your publication. Add some interesting fill effects to some of them. You might like to add an effect to the WordArt titles on your front page.
- Leave the oval with the photograph outside the publication for use later.
- Save your publication using a new filename.

Layering and grouping objects

These are two of the most useful graphics tools. They allow you to combine shapes and frames on a page, decide on the order in which they should be placed on the page, then group them together so that they behave as a single object.

You have already used layering in Chapter 9 where you changed the order of frames to allow the page number to be seen above the coloured frame in the footer. Layering is also very useful with graphic objects.

For example, if you put a photograph into a shape, as in Figure 10.15, any text will automatically **wrap** around it, making it very difficult to read.

Key term

Wrap

When a block of text adjusts so that it fits neatly around any non-text object such as a graphic.

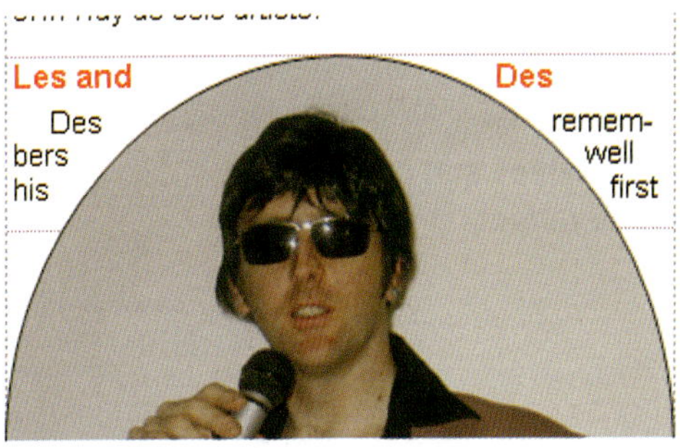

***Figure 10.15:** Putting a photograph in a shape might have an unfortunate effect on surrounding text.*

While you could overcome this problem by splitting up the text frames, this is not ideal, as it makes moving items and experimenting with layouts much more difficult. A better solution is to make a white rectangle to go behind the shape.

First make a rectangle using the rectangle tool to cover the photograph, then fill it with white and change the outline colour to white. Then right click the rectangle and choose **Order → Send Backward**. This will send the rectangle behind the photograph but leave it on top of the text, so pushing it away.

In order to keep the rectangle and shape together, so you can move them around the page together, you need to **group** them. First select all the objects you want to group. There are two main methods of selecting a number of objects at once:

- Select an object by clicking it → hold down the **Ctrl** key and select the other objects by clicking them. Notice that as you point to items, the software tells you what you are pointing at (see Figure 10.16). This can sometimes help to make sure you select the objects you want.
- Choose the **Select Objects** tool from the **Objects** toolbar and drag over the items you want to select.

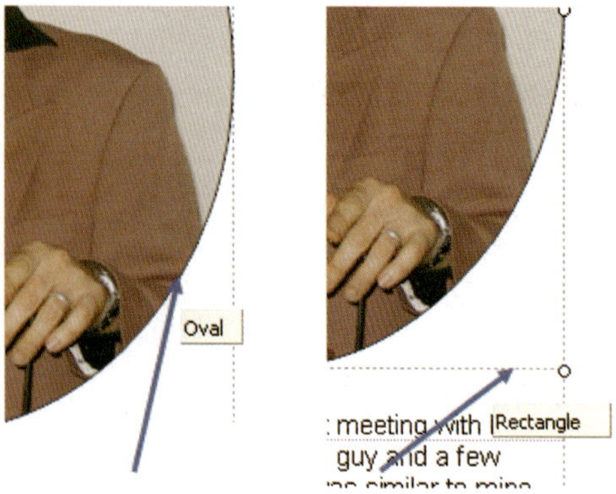

Figure 10.16: *Hovering the cursor over the edge of an object to identify it before selecting it.*

As soon as you have selected more than one object you will see a new tool at the bottom right-hand corner of the selection. This is the **Group Objects** tool . Click it to group the objects together, then if you want to ungroup them again, click the same tool. The icon will change to the **Ungroup Objects** button . Clicking the icon toggles between grouping and ungrouping.

TIP

If you want to group a set of objects together it is often easiest first to drag them all to an area outside the page. This makes it easier to select and group them. You can then drag them back into place as one object.

Activity 4: Layering and grouping...

In this activity you will:

- attach a white background to your oval photo and add it to your publication
- create a simple cartoon drawing to add to your pages.

→ Load the publication you saved at the end of Activity 3.

→ Click the oval you filled with a photograph to select it.

→ Use the **Rectangle** drawing tool to draw a rectangle over the top of the oval. Try to make it just big enough to cover the oval completely. The select handles of the oval should help you see how big the rectangle needs to be.

→ **Fill** the rectangle with **white**, then use the **Line color** tool to choose a **white** outline.

You should now not be able to see your photo.

→ With the rectangle still selected, right click and choose **Order**, then **Send backward**.

You should now be able to see your photo, sitting on top of the rectangle.

→ Use either of the methods described above to select **both** rectangle and oval. Then click the **Group objects** button.

You should now find that you can copy and paste, move and resize these two objects as if they were one.

- Find a suitable place to use this photo in your publication. You might like to replace one of your original photos with it. By creating it in the working area outside your publication pages you should find it easy to drag it to any page you like.

- Use the shapes to create a 'laughing face' cartoon. If you wish you can follow the instructions below to create the one shown in Figure 10.19. Alternatively you can create one of your own.

  - Create a circle for the outline of the face. Fill it with yellow and choose the same yellow for line colour.
  - Create a small oval for an eye. Select blue for the fill colour and line colour.
  - Copy this eye and paste to create a second, identical one. Place them in the right place on the face.
  - Use the **Moon** AutoShape to create the mouth.

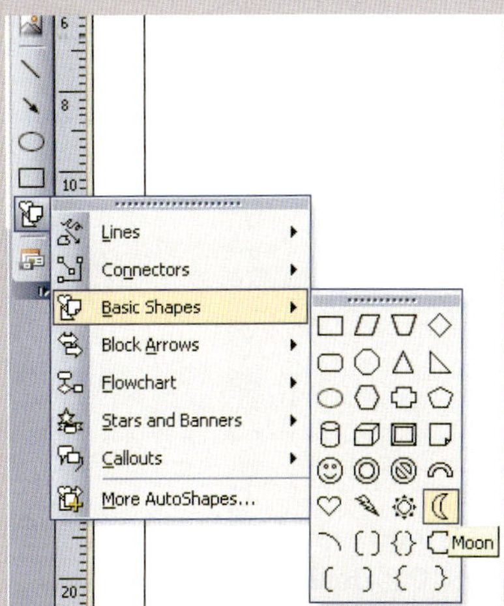

Figure 10.17: *Selecting the* ***Moon*** *AutoShape.*

  - Use the green handle to rotate the shape to the right angle.
  - Fill the mouth with a suitable gradient, then move it into place.

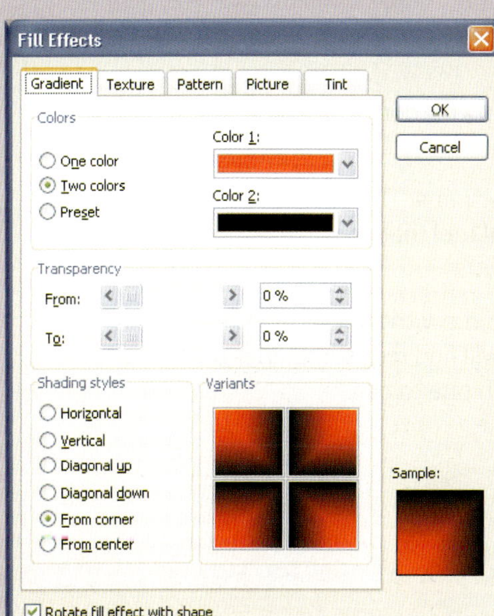

Figure 10.18: *Selecting a suitable gradient fill for the mouth.*

- Use the **Line** tool to create a short line for an eyebrow. Use the **Line/Border Style** tool to make this line thicker.
- Copy and paste this to create a second, identical eyebrow.
- Use the **Arrange** menu to choose **Rotate or Flip**, then **Flip Horizontal** to flip this second eyebrow so that it is facing the opposite way to the first.
- Make a rosy cheek from an oval shape with a yellow line style and an appropriate gradient fill from pink to yellow.
- Copy and paste this to make the second one, then flip it horizontally before moving it into place.
- Rearrange the items and make any adjustments to the face that you think are necessary.

➔ Select all the items in your cartoon and group them together.

➔ Reduce the size of your finished cartoon, so it is small enough to go on every page.

***Fig. 10.19:** The finished 'laughing face' cartoon.*

➔ Add your cartoon to a different place on every page of your publication. You might like to rotate it to different angles on different pages.

➔ Check that you have not got any text overflowing frames. You might use the **Design checker** for this, as you did in Chapter 9. If there is, you will need to edit some text or reduce the size of some graphics so that everything fits well.

➔ Save your publication, using another filename, so that you can see how it has developed.

Lines and borders

Professional publications usually make some use of lines and frame borders to separate elements on a page or to make certain items stand out.

You have already seen how to change the line/frame colour for a shape. This tool can also be used to set the style for any lines drawn. There is an additional tool that can be used to add arrowheads to a line.

Very often there are two ways of adding a line to a page. You can draw the line as an additional object or you can add a line as a border to a frame. You will find that sometimes one method is easier than another, but you can choose yourself which one to use.

Activity 5: Adding lines and borders...

In this activity you will:

- add lines by drawing them using the Line tool
- add lines by adding borders to a frame/shape
- change line/border styles, colours and widths
- change the margins within text boxes
- select different line styles for different borders on an object.

➔ Load the publication you saved at the end of Activity 4 and move to the front page.

➔ The simplest way to add a border to this page is to use the **Rectangle** tool and draw a rectangle around the page.

➔ Use the **Line color** tool to change the border to **red** and the **Line/Border Style** tool to set a line width of **3pt**.

The border of this page is only going to be at the top and right-hand edges. This now needs to be set.

➔ Right-click one edge of the border and choose **Format AutoShape...**.

➔ On the **Colors and Lines** tab click the icons for **top** and **right** edges, so that these are no longer selected. This will allow you to change the style for the left and bottom edges.

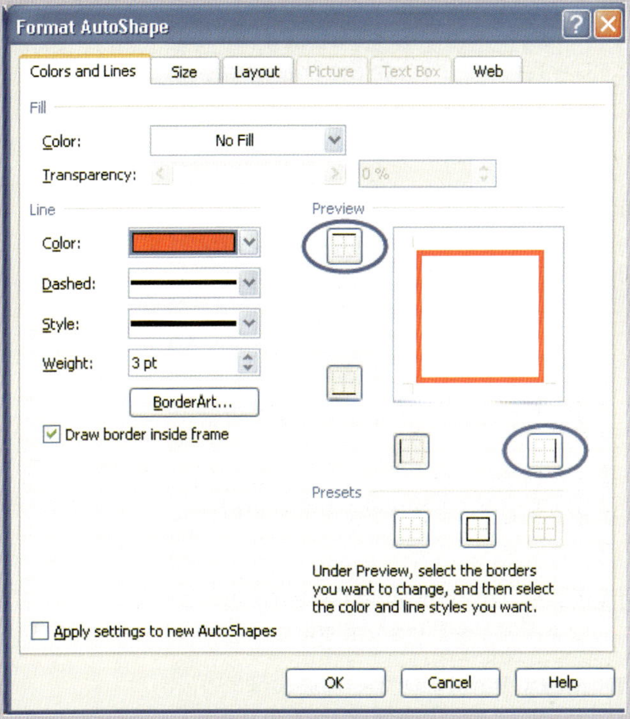

Figure 10.20: *The top and right edge icons on the Colors and Lines tab.*

➔ Use the drop-down box next to the **Line color** option to choose **No line**. This will remove the border from the remaining two sides, leaving us with the border required. Click **OK**. (See Figure 10.21.)

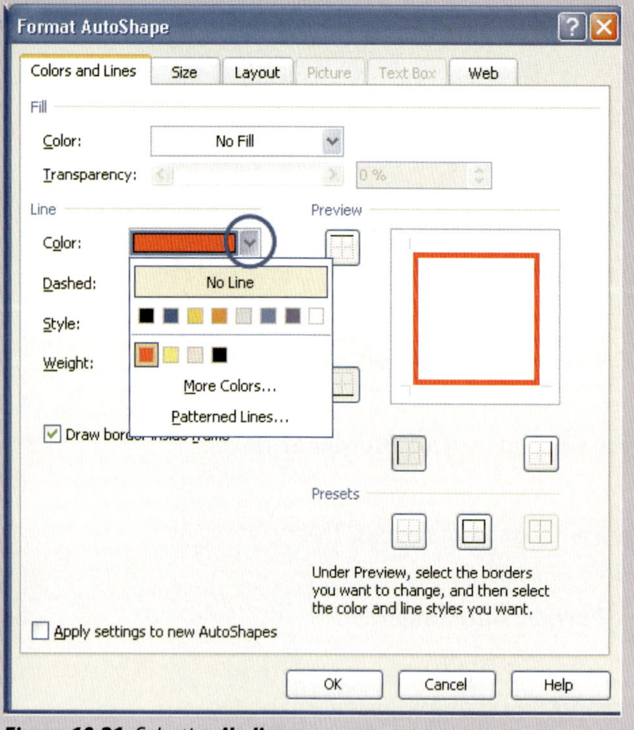

Figure 10.21: *Selecting* ***No line****.*

You now need to add appropriate borders to the rest of your pages. Although it might make sense to add these to the master pages this often results in the borders being hidden behind other items on the page, so it is usually easiest to add them to the final pages at the end.

- Move to Page 2 and add a rectangle to it.

You will find that putting a rectangle on top of a page with overlapping text and graphic frames can have an unfortunate effect on the page layout. While this can be dealt with by altering the order of objects on the page it is usually a lot easier just to add lines instead of a rectangle.

- Delete the rectangle you have just drawn.
- Use the **Line** tool to draw a line along the top edge of the page. Change the colour to **red** and the line width to **3pt**.
- Draw another line along the left-hand edge and change the colour and line width in the same way.
- Change the **Zoom** to **400%** and check the ends of each line, adjusting them as necessary until you have an accurate border. Change the zoom back again.
- Click one of your lines to select it, hold down the **Ctrl** key and click the other one. Group these together using the **Group objects** button or the **Group** option on the right-click menu.
- Copy this border and paste it on all of your other left-hand pages.

- Make another copy of the border and place it on Page 3. Click on **Arrange** on the menu bar and choose **Flip Horizontal** to put this the correct way around for a right-hand page. If the border does not flip at your first attempt, click somewhere else on the page, then select the border again and try again.
- Copy and paste this border onto all your right-hand pages.

When you add borders you may find that the text is too close to the borders. You can always change this.

- Right-click the text box at the left-hand side of Page 2. Choose **Format Text Box...**.
- Click on the **Text box** tab and increase the size of the **Left** margin.

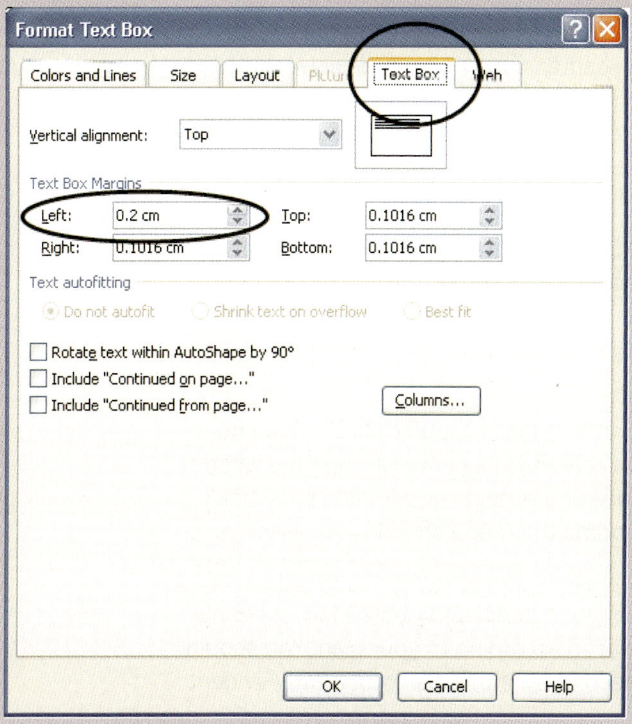

Figure 10.22: *Increasing the margin within a text box.*

- Change the margins on other pages in the same way – you will need to change the left margin of the left-hand text box on left-hand pages, then change the right margin of the right-hand text box on right-hand pages.

Another technique that is often used is to add a line between columns of text.

- Draw a line between the two text frames on Page 2. Zoom up to at least **200%** to check the position of this line and adjust it if necessary.
- If there are any graphics or quotes in the middle of the page, right click these and choose **Order** → **Bring to Front** to bring these to the front of the line, so that they cover up the line where they overlap.
- Our plan shows this line dotted rather than solid. Use the **Dash style** tool on the Formatting toolbar to choose an appropriate style. Leave the line black.

- Copy and paste this line to all the other pages that have columns of text. Make sure you bring any other graphics or quotes that overlap any of these lines to the front as before.
- Save your final publication using a new filename, and print it out.

TIP

Sometimes you will want to see what your publication looks like *without* the guidelines. Use the View menu to switch off Boundaries and Guides if you want to do this. Don't forget to put them back afterwards!

Portfolio builder

In order to gain the highest grade you must demonstrate the use of all the features listed in the 'Skills to use' section at the beginning of this chapter. You will have ideally included a use for all of these in your plan and shown them in your portfolio. However, if you didn't include them all, it is acceptable to add extra features to your publication later, so long as you explain why you think they improve the final publication. Sometimes you will need to use your imagination to find a sensible use for all of the features required!

Some features, such as layering and grouping, will be difficult to see just from looking at your final publication. You will need to take some screenshots showing these techniques being used. You should annotate these screenshots to explain what you were doing and why. You should also annotate a copy of your final publication to show where all the different features have been used.

Remember that it is up to you to show the assessor the range of graphical tools that you can use. While there is no point in producing a lot of screenshots demonstrating the same skill, you should make sure that you provide evidence of the range of skills you have used. Your grade for this Assessment Objective will depend on the range of skills your assessor can identify from your portfolio.

Your portfolio should include at least one printout of your completed publication, showing all the text and graphics correctly and accurately placed according to your plan. You should annotate this to show where different skills have been used, if these are not clearly evident from the printout alone.

You should also include in your portfolio annotated screenshots, where these help provide evidence of the skills you have used.

Check your portfolio carefully to make sure there is clear evidence for everything in the 'How to achieve' section.

CHAPTER 11

Assessment Objective 5

Prepare Publication for Print

Overview:

In this chapter you will check your publication for errors and quality. You will then print out a final proof copy. You will also find out about some of the procedures that take place between producing a proof copy and the final printing of the publication by a commercial printer.

How this assessment objective will be assessed...

The quality of your final printed publication is an important factor in assessing this objective. However, you will also need to provide a written explanation of what would happen after the proof has been produced if you were to have many copies commercially printed. The detail and completeness of this explanation will also contribute to your assessment. In order to pass this assessment objective you will need to produce a covering letter to send with your proof, although the quality of this letter will not be assessed.

Skills to use...

There are no additional DTP skills needed for this objective. What is important is care and attention to detail when checking your final publication, to make sure that it is of the highest possible quality, and free from errors.

How to achieve...

Pass requirements

P1 You will print a final proof copy of your publication.

P2 There will be a covering letter.

P3 You will provide a brief outline of the final stages of producing multiple copies using commercial printing processes.

Merit requirements

M1 You will print a final proof copy of your publication that will not contain many errors.

M2 There will be a covering letter.

M3 The overall quality of the document will be good.

M4 You will provide an outline of all the final stages of producing multiple copies using commercial printing processes.

Distinction requirements

D1 You will print a final proof copy of your publication that will be mostly free from errors.

D2 There will be a covering letter.

D3 The overall quality of the document will be near to business standard.

D4 You will provide a detailed outline of all the final stages of producing multiple copies using commercial printing processes.

Final quality checks

When producing a document using DTP techniques it is easy for errors to be made. Some common errors are:

- typing errors – spelling and other typographical errors in the text
- text overflowing frames, so that the last line or two are missing on the printed document
- graphics that are stretched out of proportion
- hyphenation that the software has automatically created, but which looks odd
- widows and orphans, including titles that are separated from the text they refer to
- lines and shapes that don't exactly meet where they should, when viewed at full size
- overlapping shapes that are not layered in the right order, so that, for example, a line goes through the middle of a picture when it should be behind it
- pages that look too crowded and/or too busy
- pages with large gaps where there is no content.

In order to minimise errors you should carry out the following:

- Use the Spelling tool to automatically check for spelling errors. Remember that there is no grammar checker in Publisher. If you know that your grammar is not very good, and you usually rely on the grammar checker in a word processor, you can always copy and paste text into a word processor, check it and then copy and paste it back into your publication.
- Use the Design checker tool to automatically check for text overflowing frames and graphics stretched out of proportion.
- Carefully read through your publication, checking for any other types of error in the text. Remember that spell checkers only check that the words you have used are in the dictionary – they don't check that they are the correct ones! If you find any errors you will need to correct them.
- Minimise occurrences of widows and orphans by using the appropriate **Line and Paragraph Breaks** options in each of the styles used. However, it is still important to check that no mistakes have been made. If necessary, line breaks can usually be adjusted manually by slightly adjusting the size of graphics or the margins within text frames. Alternatively, a strategically placed white rectangle with no outline can sometimes be used, or a text frame simply shortened.
- Remove hyphenation by using **Tools** → **Language** → **Hyphenation...**.
- Remember that whenever you make a change you will need to check that you haven't introduced any other errors. For example, removing hyphenation might change the number of lines of text, so creating new widows/orphans or making text overflow a frame.

- Zoom in on your publication to check graphics carefully.
- Print out a copy and check it – it is often surprising how many errors you can find on paper that you miss when looking on screen.
- Ask at least one other person to check your publication for errors and to make any comments about its layout – it is likely that they will see errors that you keep missing.
- If you are preparing your publication for a client you must give them a **proof copy** for their approval. This will allow them to let you know of any changes they require.

Key terms

Line breaks

The point at which a line of text breaks and forms a new line.

Proof copy

A printed copy of the publication which is checked for any errors or changes before the publication is printed in bulk.

If you are going to have multiple copies of your document printed it is absolutely essential that you check it very carefully before printing these copies. Whether you are printing them yourself at home or having them commercially printed, a simple mistake that could have been easily corrected on a proof copy can be extremely expensive to correct later, and could prevent you having your final copies ready on time.

Saving your publication for use on another computer system

If you are going to use a commercial printing company to print your publication it is *possible* that they might be able to print from Publisher files. However, you cannot assume that they will have exactly the same fonts as you have on your computer. Publisher offers a tool to export your publication with any associated fonts and linked files, so that it can be read on any system that can read Publisher files.

For the purpose of this unit you can assume that you will be having your publication printed by a company that can work with Publisher files, even though you will also have to know about the alternative options that are explained later in this chapter.

You should ensure your publication is in its final form and save it normally. Then choose **File → Pack and Go → Take to a Commercial Printing Service...**. You are then asked for a suitable location for the files that will be produced. This will normally be a CD, as this is the most convenient medium for sending to a printing company. For the purpose of this unit you can simply use a separate folder within your usual work area.

At the end of the Pack and Go process you are offered the opportunity to print a proof copy. This will print a **composite proof** – one which prints all the elements on the pages, as you would expect. Other options that might be needed for commercial printing are discussed later.

Activity 1: Preparing a publication for a commercial printer...

In this activity you will:

- carry out checks on your publication
- pack your publication for transporting to another computer system
- print out a final proof copy.

Load the final version of your publication, saved at the end of Chapter 10.

Use **Tools** → **Spelling** → **Spelling...** to check your text for spelling errors.

Use **Tools** → **Design Checker...** to check your publication for common layout errors such as stretched pictures or text overflowing frames.

Look carefully through each page and check that you have no widows or orphans.

Now read through all of the text and make sure that it all makes sense. Look out for any hyphenation that might look a bit strange. If you want to change the hyphenation, use **Tools** → **Language** → **Hyphenation...** and uncheck the **Automatically hyphenate this story** box. If you then click **OK**, all hyphenation will be removed for the text in the selected set of linked frames. Alternatively, click on the **Manual...** button and you can then choose whether or not to accept each occurrence of hyphenation in that piece of text.

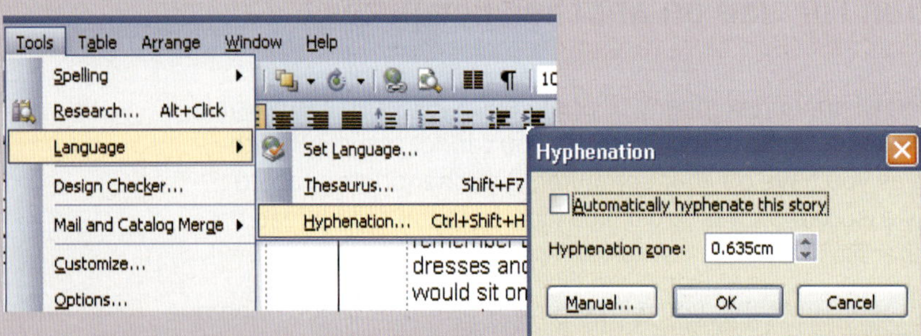

***Figure 11.1:** The **Hyphenation** dialogue box.*

Make sure that you can see the layout guides on the pages. If not, use **View** → **Boundaries and Guides** to make these visible. Change the **Zoom** to at least 100% and check the edges of frames, lines and graphics. For some items you will need to zoom in further to be absolutely sure they are in the correct place. Make any adjustments that are necessary.

Save your publication if you have made any changes, then print out a copy.

Read through carefully, looking especially at general features of layout. Ask yourself if any of the pages are too 'busy' or if any of the white space is excessive. Mark any corrections that are needed on your printout.

Show your printout to at least one other person and ask them for any comments.

Make any additional improvements that are necessary and save your final file.

- Click on **File** on the menu bar and choose **Pack and Go**, then **Take to a Commercial Printing Service**. Follow the wizard's instructions, choosing a suitable location for the files. Since you do not actually need to take these files anywhere, it is quite acceptable to save them in the same location as the original file, although it is a good idea to use the **Browse** button and create a new folder for these files, to separate them from all your other files. Accept all the options on the final screen.
- When the Pack and Go process is complete, accept the option to print your publication. This will be your final proof copy.

Commercial printing

For the purpose of this unit you do not need to actually have your publication commercially printed, but you do need to be aware of the final stages involved in producing multiple copies of your publication using a commercial printing company. These companies will most likely use one of two types of printing technology:

- Digital printing. This is essentially a very fast, high-volume laser printer. This is suitable for relatively small print runs (less than 500 sheets) because, although it will be a lot faster than a personal laser printer, it is much slower than the alternative, more traditional, printing methods and is likely to be more expensive for large quantities.
- Offset lithography. This prints using plates each inked in a single colour, with multiple plates used to create the range of colours required. It is called 'offset' because the paper never touches the plates themselves: the ink is transferred from the plates to a rubber 'blanket', from where it is transferred to the paper. Creating these plates is expensive so this is not a realistic option for short print runs. Before computers were used to create and set the plates the set-up costs were even greater, meaning that print runs of less than several thousand were not cost-effective.

Quantity	250	500	750	1000	1500	2000	2500	3000	Cost per additional 1000
Offset Litho	£500	£525	£550	£575	£625	£675	£725	£775	£105
Digital	£310	£535	£755	£975	£1,410	£1,850	£2,285	£2,725	£875

***Figure 11.2:** Example 2007 prices for digital printing and offset lithography.*

Preparing documents for commercial printing

The key to producing a document for commercial printing is to find a suitable printing company and discuss requirements before you begin. Prices and options may differ considerably between companies, depending on the technology used. Choices you will need to make include:

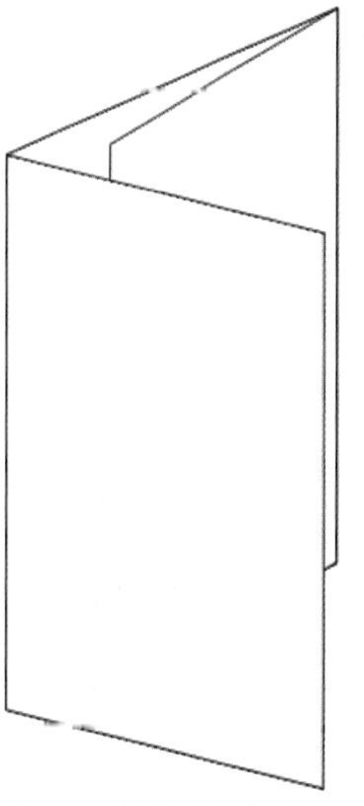

***Figure 11.3:** A C-fold document.*

- The number of pages you will have in your publication. Obviously the more pages you have, the more it will cost. You need to make sure from the outset that you are preparing the correct number of pages for your needs, which includes your budget!
- The type of fold you will have. An A4 document is likely to be produced using folded A3 sheets, sometimes printed on both sides. However, by using different types of fold you can have different numbers of pages. A common alternative is **C fold**, which allows a document to have six pages. You may have used Publisher templates that produce a folded leaflet from a single A4 sheet using a C fold. With a larger paper size,

the equivalent of three A4 pages, a six-page leaflet/newsletter can be produced. You may have seen publications using different types of fold. A commercial printer might suggest suitable fold types for a particular publication and will possibly have different prices for different styles.

- The type of paper/card you require. Paper can be bought in different qualities and thicknesses. 80 **gsm** is the standard weight paper that is normally used for general printing purposes. However, commercial leaflets and publications are usually produced on heavier weight papers. Indeed, one of the most obvious differences between professional documents and home-produced ones is often the quality and weight of paper used. As well as the weight you can also choose between matt or glossy paper. Again, these choices will depend partly on the purpose of your document and what you want it to look like, and partly on your budget. You will also need to choose the colour of paper to use. You would probably be surprised to find out that there are even many different shades of white paper!
- The number of colours you will use. The cheapest option is to print just using black ink. Colour can then be provided by using coloured paper or card. The next option is to choose **spot printing**, which will allow shades of one or more colours in addition to black, requiring one extra plate for each extra colour. For example, you might choose to have a document using black and red ink. This will allow you to have black and white photographs and to use shades of red for graphics, text, backgrounds, etc. The more colours you have the more plates you will need and the more the printing will cost. For a full-colour document, such as the one you have created in this chapter, you would need to use **process printing**, which uses four colours (Cyan, Magenta, Yellow and Black (key plate), referred to as CMYK). This is more expensive, but is capable of producing a range of colours (as required for colour photographs) by printing each of these colours separately and producing different shades and colours by mixing tiny dots of the different colours on the page. For the purpose of this unit you have created a full-colour publication, but in real life you would first research the print options, then create a publication that matches your needs and your budget.

Key term

gsm

Grams per square metre. A measurement of the thickness of paper – thicker paper will be heavier.

File types

Although you may find a printing company that will accept Microsoft Publisher files, this is not a standard software application for the publishing industry. Many commercial printers use Apple Macintosh computers and/or cannot accept Publisher files. The companies will have many customers using a wide range of different software, so it is unrealistic to expect them to support all of them.

The printing company will tell you how they would like you to provide your final document. If the company does not accept Publisher files, they are likely to ask either for a **PostScript** file or a **pdf** file.

- A **PostScript** file is a file in a format that cannot be edited but which can be used by other computers regardless of any DTP software they might, or might not, have. A PostScript file defines the layout and content of each page in a form that is independent of the software used to create it.
- A **pdf** (portable document format) file is a file produced by specialist software, which shows the layout of the page, again not requiring the original software to show this.

Microsoft Publisher offers an option to save as a PostScript file, although you will need a Post-Script printer driver, but if you need your file in pdf format you will need additional software (e.g. Adobe Acrobat Distiller) – the printing company may give you a special printer driver to create a file in this format for them to read. There are other applications available that can create pdf files, but these are not all in a form that a commercial printing company can use.

Printer drivers – a warning

Publisher is different from many other applications in that it takes account of the selected printer driver when setting up page margins. You may have had experience in school or college of creating a document, printing it in black and white, then printing it on a colour printer and finding that the objects don't fit on the page in exactly the same way.

As explained in Chapter 9, it is important, when using Publisher, to select the printer driver you are going to use as soon as you start your new publication, **before** you do anything else. Do this using **File** → **Page Setup...** → **Printer and Paper**. If you create a publication that needs to be given to a printing company as a PostScript file, you will need to select the PostScript printer driver at this point: this means that if you do not have a PostScript printer, then all your proof-reading before creating your final copy wil have to be done on screen.

Delivering your publication to a commercial printing company

When you have completed the final version of your publication and are absolutely sure it is error-free you need to deliver the files and a proof print to the printing company. It is impossible to overemphasise the importance of ensuring the document is 100% correct before delivery, as changes made afterwards can be very expensive.

You should already have discussed a deadline with the company. When you told them what you would require and when you would need the final printed documents they would have told you when they would need the files by. It is a good idea to try to get these in a few days before, so that any problems can be sorted out without affecting your final deadline.

You can deliver the file to the company on CD or by email. Once again, it is likely that you will negotiate this with the company, to find out their preferred option. The file(s) will be either those produced by Publisher's Pack and Go wizard or will be in PostScript or pdf format, according to the requirements of the printing company.

You should also supply a high-quality **black and white** printout of your completed publication. Even if you are using a colour printer this is possible by selecting **Print** → **Advanced Printing Settings...** and choosing the **Composite Grayscale** output option.

If you have a PostScript printer driver and require a colour print then you should also supply printouts in **colour separation** mode, that is one printout for each colour plate to be used. This option is available from Publisher when you have the required driver software installed.

You should write an accompanying letter to confirm all other details such as:

- your name and contact details
- the name/type of the publication
- the paper required, e.g. size, colour, weight and whether or not it is to be glossy
- any folding, stapling, stitching, etc. that is needed
- the type of printing required, i.e. digital or offset lithography
- the type of colour printing required, e.g. black only, spot printing (specify additional colours), CMYK process printing
- the date by which you require the final printed copies
- how you want the final copies to be delivered to you or whether you will arrange to have them collected.

As all of these details will have been negotiated beforehand there is no need to go into any great detail, but it is important to ensure they are all confirmed at this stage. You will probably have a contract or agreement letter that you can refer to, which should prevent you forgetting anything.

When the company receives your files and instructions the plates will be made (unless digital printing is to be used) and one copy will be printed. This is the final proof for you to check, which will be sent to you. Some companies will offer a proof copy as an option, but it is a very important stage, as it is your only chance to see the document in its final form before the bulk copies are printed.

Normally you would hope that no changes will be needed, as these are likely to cost extra unless it is an error on the part of the printer. However, you need to check carefully to ensure margins, colours, fonts, etc. are correct and that photographs have been printed correctly. Any changes that are needed to the content will need to be made to the original document and then a new file in the correct format will need to be created and submitted. Although the commercial printer can do some text editing, it is usually better to make text corrections in the original file. Again, this is something that will need to be discussed with the company.

After checking the final proof you will send back to the company their proofs (with any changes clearly marked using standard proofing symbols), any corrected files and accompanying instructions.

Key term

Proofing symbols

These are a set of standard symbols used by editors and publishers. They ensure that any corrections or changes can be efficiently marked up and clearly communicated to the person who implements the changes in the original file.

If any changes have been made then completely new offset lithography plates will need to be made for the altered pages. This will obviously add to your cost. The copies will then be made and the final documents folded, stapled, etc. as required. You will then receive these, with the invoice from the company.

An example of an appropriate covering letter is shown in Figure 11.4.

OXK Design
4 Illustrator Avenue
OXFORD
OX4 8FX

1 September 2007

Halley Court Printers
Jordan Crescent
OXFORD
OX2 8RG

Dear Sir,

Les and Des Return to Laughter Programme

Further to our conversations and agreement of 30 June 2007 please find enclosed a CD and printed copy of the final draft of the above programme. As agreed this CD contains files exported from Microsoft Publisher, which can be extracted by double-clicking on the file **unpack.exe**.

I would like to confirm the following details:

- The programme is to be printed on A3 100gsm white glossy paper, folded and stapled to form an 8-page A4 booklet.
- 8000 copies are required.
- Printing is to be full colour CMYK process printing.
- Proof copy to be delivered to me by post at the above address by 20 September.
- I will return proofs by 27 September.
- Final copies to be ready for collection by me on 15 October.

I hope that you will find everything in order and look forward to hearing from you. If you have any queries please do not hesitate to contact me on ak@oxkdesign.co.uk or 01865 880065.

Yours faithfully,

Anne Kelsall

Figure 11.4: *An example of a covering letter to accompany your publication.*

Activity 2: The covering letter...

In this activity you will write a covering letter to a printing company to go with your files.

You have created an eight-page programme for Les and Des. This is to be sent to:

Mr M Marston
P&D Printing Ltd
North Street
Southlands
Anyshire
CM42 7YK

You have agreed with the company that it will print 2000 copies on 130 gsm white glossy paper, using CMYK process printing. The printing is to be done on A3 paper, folded and stapled to form an eight-page programme. You have agreed that the proof copy will be sent to you one week after submitting the files, which you are enclosing on CD in pdf format. You have also agreed that any changes will be submitted by you within three days of receiving the proofs, and that the final programmes will be delivered to you by courier within two weeks of this.

- Write a letter to the company to accompany the CD and printed copy (which you do not have to create). Make sure you include all the necessary information, calculating actual dates from the date of the letter.
- Remember to include the standard information that needs to go on every business letter: your details, the date, the name and address of the person you are writing to, an appropriate salutation (Dear Mr Marston) and an appropriate complimentary close (Yours sincerely).

Portfolio builder

For your own portfolio you will need to ensure you carry out all necessary final quality checks to ensure your publication is the very best quality possible. This is the most significant factor that will affect the grade you achieve in this objective.

You will need to include a printout of your final publication. Although in reality the proof you send to a commercial printer is likely to be in black and white, for assessment purposes your final printout will be much better in colour. However, you can also submit your electronic Publisher file for assessment, if your centre agrees.

You will need to write a covering letter covering the main points outlined in this chapter. Although the quality of the letter itself will not be assessed you must include all necessary points, as this will demonstrate your understanding of the processes involved in producing multiple copies using a commercial printer.

You will then need to include a report giving details of the stages that are needed from the completion of your final document to the production of multiple copies by a commercial printer. The level of detail and accuracy of this report will also help determine your final grade. The information provided in this chapter should be sufficient to enable you to produce this report. However, you may also wish to carry out further research on the Internet or by contacting printing companies, to find out exactly what a particular company requires.

Index